PRAISE FOR PASTOR TIM'S BOOK

I am so excited about The Vision of Nehemiah, God's Plan for Righteous Living *and how it will encourage you to rebuild the wall or ministry that God has called you to do, just like He did with Nehemiah. It also gives a very practical understanding on helping others to walk out their faith.*

Roger Audorff
Missions Director
South Texas Assemblies of God Ministries
Serving 26 years in Foreign and U.S. Missions

Dr. Tim Barker and I have been friends since the 1980s. We have worked together in ministry for many years. He is a passionate, faithful man of God.

I enjoyed The Vision of Nehemiah, God's Plan for Righteous Living. *Dr. Barker has provided an excellent Bible study. I highly recommend this study for personal spiritual enrichment, a small group study, or a sermon series. His book has inspired me to stay in God's will and always do my part.*

Rev. Tammy Calderon
Church Ministries and Discipleship Director
South Texas Assemblies of God Ministries

Experience adds color and depth to our life. It also *clarifies and widens our insight, understanding and application of God's Word to living as well as ministry. Dr. Tim Barker certainly has walked through and lived in many circumstances and ministry positions that have often landed him in pressure cooker situations that not too many experience. It is there that the Word of God, living and active, finds places in which to bring healing, direction, and applied wisdom that escape others. Also, Tim is a faithful, loving husband, father and grandfather! Talk about adding color and depth to life!*

It is out of serving others, leading leaders, excellent education, a great family and life experience that the richness of this book flows! The Book of Nehemiah comes to life through the lenses of Dr. Barker's life. This is a must read! You will discover freshness and a broadening of your ability to apply the Word to everyday living and leading!

I can say without hesitation, this man is the real deal. A person of genuine Godly character who is the same person whether leading, speaking or watching his grandson play ball. For me, that adds such a powerful dimension to The Vision of Nehemiah, God's Plan for Righteous Living.

Pastor Wayne Clark
Senior Adult Director
South Texas Assemblies of God Ministries

A life changing adventure through the book of Nehemiah accompanied with biblical, spiritual and life-changing wisdom. Dr. Tim Barker helps explore the relativity of the scripture in our lives grounded on his vision of Health, Growth and Development. This book provides much needed nutrition by absorbing a mix of the lessons found in the book of Nehemiah with real life stories of overcoming. As I journey this life helping churches reach their full potential, I see the importance of learning from examples others have experienced in life. Dr. Tim brings to life the profound example of Nehemiah for us to use today. Wow, What a read!

Jim Kautz Jr.
Church Health Director and U.S. Missions
South Texas Assemblies of God Ministries

A book is no greater than the life behind the author. I have known Superintendent Tim Barker since his university days when it was a high honor of mine to have him as a student in class. He steeped himself in the Word of God, in Scripture memorization and lived a life in the fires of the altar. An acquaintance is one thing—watching one over a lifetime is quite another. Superintendent Barker's walk with God is a lifetime in God. He well defines consistency, stickability and maintenance of the fire of the Holy Spirit in his paradigm life of deep prayer. If you can only read one book besides the Bible this year, make it this one. Its contents are attuned to the times we are living in. Help is on the way through this timeless book. You will find an anchor and your grounding in this read.

Dr. Adonna Otwell
Chair, Department of General Studies
Southwestern Assemblies of God University
Ordained Minister with the Assemblies of God

Dr. Timothy R. Barker's in-depth study of the Book of Nehemiah is a needed instruction manual for the hour in which we live and is a road map that guides us to action facilitating healing to an individual, a church or a nation. Dr. Barker challenges us to take courage and step out to do God's will. As the pain of sin drove Nehemiah to prayer, fasting, humility and action, so let it be that our lives will become the answer through serving those we are around.

Don K. Wiehe
Executive Secretary Treasurer
South Texas Assemblies of God Ministries

THE VISION OF
NEHEMIAH
GOD'S PLAN FOR RIGHTEOUS LIVING

THE VISION OF
NEHEMIAH
GOD'S PLAN FOR RIGHTEOUS LIVING

Tim R. Barker, D. Min.

Superintendent of the South Texas
District of the Assemblies of God

Tim R. Barker Ministries

THE VISION OF NEHEMIAH, Barker, Tim.
1st ed.

Formatting, proofing, and cover provided by:
Farley Dunn
of
Three Skillet Publishing
◗✿◗ THREE SKILLET
www.ThreeSkilletPublishing.com

Tim R. Barker Ministries

ISBN: 978-1-7358529-0-4

DEDICATED TO:

THE SOUTH TEXAS ASSEMBLIES OF GOD MINISTRY CENTER

Just as Nehemiah extolled the virtues of MINISTRY through PRAISE and WORSHIP, we desire to PREPARE in FAITHFULNESS and THANKFULNESS to reach South Texas and the WORLD for Jesus!

TABLE OF CONTENTS

Foreword

Remember me, my God, for good, according to all that I have done for this people (Nehemiah 5:19, NKJV). Nehemiah expressed these words, conveying a deep sentiment that resided within his heart. Like each and every one of us, Nehemiah desired that his life would be memorable and respected. And Nehemiah's words and works have indeed been remembered as part of the world's most read and most sacred text, the Bible.

Approximately 2400 years later, again Nehemiah's words, "Remember me," have been recalled through the special focus in Dr. Tim Barker's excellent work, *The Vision of Nehemiah: God's Plan for Righteous Living*. After reading his commentary about Nehemiah, I thought – no doubt – if Nehemiah could have read this book, he would have said, "Hmmm, I didn't realize so many profound and practical truths could be derived from my wall-building days."

Dr. Barker's book is an expository study that deals with true, real-life circumstances pertaining to leadership and the qualities that are absolutely essential if people are going to trust in a leader's vision and plan. Preparation, balance, courage, discouragement, distractions, and determination are merely a few of the discussed issues a leader will encounter.

As a friend and colleague to Tim for many years, I

have witnessed his ministry progress from the early years through the present prominent position of leadership that he holds today. I can truly say, "Tim understands the role of leadership and 'follow-ship.'" So in this book, Tim offers his insight into the process of becoming a leader and then continuing as a leader. He combines his personal experiences with multiple historical allusions and examples, ranging from military personalities, to business entrepreneurs, to biblical figures for a full perspective.

This work is a motivational and inspirational study of Nehemiah presented in an illuminating, verse-by-verse, chapter-by-chapter approach. However, this book is not limited to theoretical concepts and premises, but it conveys practical application for every person who aspires to be a leader or who currently serves in such a capacity.

Nehemiah was remembered for the good that he had done. I believe that Dr. Tim Barker's time and energy in writing this book will also be remembered for the good that he has done in sharing his thoughts and insights in this book.

Danny Alexander, Ph.D.
Ordained Minister and Professor
Southwestern Assemblies of God University

It Takes

Determination

Nehemiah 1:1-4

The words of Nehemiah son of Hakaliah:

In the month of Kislev in the twentieth year, while I was in the citadel of Susa, Hanani, one of my brothers, came from Judah with some other men, and I questioned them about the Jewish remnant that had survived the exile, and also about Jerusalem.

They said to me, "Those who survived the exile and are back in the province are in great trouble and disgrace. The wall of Jerusalem is broken down, and its gates have been burned with fire."

When I heard these things, I sat down and

wept. For some days I mourned and fasted and prayed before the God of heaven.

One of the more difficult aspects of God's will is not so much *knowing* it as it is *doing* it!

How does one accomplish God's will? What is it that makes a man or woman a great man or woman of God? You will never know God's great rewards unless you are willing to take the great risks involved in doing God's will.

Look back through the annals of history. The great leaders we remember today are the men and women who took calculated risks – *never foolish gambles* – that at times endangered life and limb, yet that also promised every chance of fantastic success.

Great courage offers the possibility of great pay-offs:

- *Columbus' voyage revealed a whole new world.*
- *Man's voyage to the moon established man's mark in space.*
- *Paul's ministry brought the gospel to the West and the world.*
- *The ministry and life of Jesus changed twelve men's lives (and so many more!).*
- *Gideon's call to fight with only 300 men against*

a huge army proved God's promises!

- *And that's only skimming the surface of what's possible when we exercise courage!*

Why not go out on a limb? Isn't that where the fruit is? – an expression found in many self-help books, thought to be originally coined by Frank Scully, journalist.

You will never do anything for God if you don't have courage and take some risks! *It takes guts to do God's will* ... those without determination can't make it in the kingdom, or they will remain fruitless in their walk with God!

Our Example of Courage

Nehemiah is our Biblical example of a man of God who revealed courage that came from God and a determination to step out on that courage, even if he had to twist some arms along the way.

At the beginning of this passage, Nehemiah expresses *concern* (vv. 1-2), which leads to a *partnership*:

> *One of my brothers and some other men came ...* (v. 2)

It's important to understand the context of Nehemiah's concern about Jerusalem and his ancestral homeland. Let's step back 100 years to the time of Cyrus, the Great King of All Kings.

Ezra 1:1, 3 in the King James Version tells us: "In the first year of Cyrus king of Persia … he made a proclamation … [to] build the house of the LORD God of Israel, which is in Jerusalem."

Many years before Cyrus' proclamation, Solomon's temple had been destroyed. Following Cyrus' decree, a group of Israelites returned to Jerusalem and began the rebuilding.

After the altar and the foundation were in place, the people grew tired of laboring on the temple when life was hard in other areas. It took Haggai and Zechariah to encourage the people to complete the temple.

Ezra, Nehemiah's predecessor, came along and began to point the Israelites back to holiness, worship, and righteous living as defined by the Law of Moses.

Even so, the once prosperous city remained desolate and sparsely populated. Much of her people still lived in captivity, with their pride in Jerusalem's history and their spirit of independence decimated by their years of slavery.

This set the stage for Nehemiah. He learned of Jerusalem's deplorable condition and received a mandate from the Lord: the children of Israel needed one another.

God had set the stage for their return and Jerusalem's restoration.

Next, Nehemiah expresses pain (vv. 3-4). Upon learning that all was not well in Jerusalem, Nehemiah's heart was broken!

This is the kind of man God can use! The first part of courage is starting to reveal itself. *Brokenness* is the foundation for *courage!*

Think of it this way: A ship in harbor is safe, but that is not what ships are for. It is only when we journey into the open sea – with all the dangers that entails – that a ship comes into its own.

Nehemiah 1:5-9

Then I said:

"Lord, the God of heaven, the great and awesome God, who keeps his covenant of love with those who love him and keep his commandments, let your ear be attentive and your eyes open to hear the prayer your servant is

praying before you day and night for your servants, the people of Israel. I confess the sins we Israelites, including myself and my father's family, have committed against you. We have acted very wickedly toward you. We have not obeyed the commands, decrees and laws you gave your servant Moses.

"Remember the instruction you gave your servant Moses, saying, 'If you are unfaithful, I will scatter you among the nations, but if you return to me and obey my commands, then even if your exiled people are at the farthest horizon, I will gather them from there and bring them to the place I have chosen as a dwelling for my Name.'"

A Prayer for Forgiveness

Nehemiah is so broken over the news that he begins to weep and fast ... a Biblical fast! He was fasting because the burden was so great that food was unimportant! (He was not fasting to pressure God or manipulate Him. Pressuring God is not the purpose of a Biblical fast!)

Nehemiah was in pain, and there are always two reactions to pain: bitterness and anger. It's easy to feel that God has cheated you – this kind of reaction goes on to produce bitterness!

The better choice is to take on the burden in prayer – this goes on to produce a courageous saint!

The response we choose is up to us. Pain is never fun, but it can be the *first stage* toward great blessing!

Lastly is *confession*, and that happens when the pain becomes personal (vv. 5-7). It generates a personal prayer, not for the release of pain, but for personal forgiveness!

This is the second great quality of courage: *humility! This is humility born in prayerfulness!*

Nehemiah could have blamed his brethren for all their misery. He could have said, "If only they had not been so stubborn of heart, then we wouldn't be here now!"

Instead, Nehemiah starts with himself! This was no careless prayer ... the burden was too great. Nehemiah determined he would pray until he felt resolve within his own spirit!

He doesn't have an answer to the problem *yet*, but he *is* on the right track!

Nehemiah has revealed an important truth: Sometimes praying is NOT for an answer but to prepare us to BE THE ANSWER!

A New Way Forward

How would God solve this major problem with Israel's powerlessness in captivity? Nehemiah in his prayer for Israel's forgiveness doesn't *blame* them. He *intercedes* for them.

Notice the promise that is expressed in verses 8-9. Fortunately, Nehemiah knows God's Word and knows the faithfulness of God! This is the third phase of courage, knowing God's character and *trusting him*.

Nehemiah was not so much reminding God of His promise as he was reminding himself of God's character to restore a remnant of His people! In other words, he was counting God as *faithful!* This gives us the fourth characteristic of courage: *hope*.

Nehemiah 1:10-11

"They are your servants and your people, whom you redeemed by your great strength and your mighty hand. Lord, let your ear be attentive to the prayer of this your servant and to the prayer of your servants who delight in revering your name. Give your servant success today by granting him favor in the presence of this man."

I was cupbearer to the king.

Promise to Petition

Nehemiah then moves from promise to petition (vv. 10-11). After reminding himself of God's faithfulness, he feels enough courage to ask God for an answer.

Notice that his request of God includes his own willingness to *be the channel used by God*.

This is the fifth step of courage: *availability*. While Nehemiah is asking God for help, he is preparing himself to be used, if needed! It is not enough to ask God for help if you are unwilling to be used if He calls you.

The final sentence of chapter one finally reveals the emerging courage Nehemiah really has: *"I was cupbearer to the king."*

Nehemiah was actually a nobody, but he was ready to get involved, anyway! A simple servant is all he was ... wait! Perhaps that is the secret!

Today, modern kingdom authority teachers would likely tell Nehemiah to just shout at the king and state: *"I am God's servant, and I take authority over you!"*

Not Nehemiah ... he understood real kingdom authority! Carefully notice the wording of this last verse: Nehemiah was a servant to the *real king* ... he states he *"delights in revering God's name!"*

Nehemiah's Real King

Nehemiah's real king is GOD ... and he is but a servant!

Notice his perspective of the earthly king. Nehemiah calls him but a *"man!"* But he is not disrespectful of the position of the earthly king! His request was for God to give him favor as *a simple cupbearer* to an earthly king. After all, what could happen ... only the possibility of having his head removed or something similar! In those days, you did not speak to an earthly king unless he spoke to you first.

Aren't you glad God is different?

How would Nehemiah get this king to ask him about his concern for Jerusalem? We now have revealed the sixth characteristic of courage: *creative solutions.*

Nehemiah 2:1-3

In the month of Nisan in the twentieth year of King Artaxerxes, when wine was brought for him, I took the wine and gave it to the king. I

had not been sad in his presence before, so the
king asked me, "Why does your face look so
sad when you are not ill? This can be nothing
but sadness of heart."

I was very much afraid, but I said to the king,
"May the king live forever! Why should my face
not look sad when the city where my ancestors
are buried lies in ruins, and its gates have been
destroyed by fire?"

A Courageous Solution

Nehemiah's position takes real *courage*, as we see in chapter 2:1-3.

When God calls you to minister, He often uses you right where you are, using the skills you already have! Nehemiah couldn't ask the king outright ... he was but a servant.

However, the king had to look him in the eye every time Nehemiah served him his cup. It was simple for Nehemiah to look sad and distressed. The king would notice because it wasn't Nehemiah's usual look!

Had Nehemiah been like many Christians today – who walk around most of the time like the devil has won – the king might not have noticed his sadness.

The reason the king noticed Nehemiah's sad look was that it was *not common for Nehemiah!* And so, Nehemiah used his lowly position as servant to try and save his own nation ... *These are always the best fighters, the ones who are already servants and humble!* He was already in the position he needed to be in to be used of God in a great way ... as a humble and a faithful servant!

Just Like Us

It is nice to know that Nehemiah is also very much like us. Take, for example, his reaction to being able to present his petition to the king. This helps us to understand Biblical courage. It is okay to be scared, and it is okay be honest about it ... *but don't quit.* Nehemiah stood before the king. It was the crucial point of his participation in God's plan. Would Nehemiah's godly courage hold out?

Here are the two steps Nehemiah takes to hold fast to his courage.

1. He is first of all polite. He understands that having courage doesn't mean we must be demanding!

2. Secondly, he explains the honesty of his sadness and his concern over the brokenness of Jerusalem. It

is noteworthy that he faced his fear honestly but didn't give in to it!

We see the seventh characteristic of courage: *honesty with durability.*

We must face head-on into whatever frightening or overwhelming situation we face. Think of a ship at sea in a storm. The ship turns bow first into the storm. If the ship turns aside, the waves will capsize it. If it tries to run from the storm or turn its back to the storm, the wind can drive it onto the rocks.

We must *face the storm to find safety in the storm.*

It is important that when the king asks Nehemiah what it was that he wanted from the king, Nehemiah had already *planned his response!* The eighth characteristic of courage is *preparedness.*

Nehemiah 2:4-10

The king said to me, "What is it you want?"

Then I prayed to the God of heaven, and I answered the king, "If it pleases the king and if your servant has found favor in his sight, let him send me to the city in Judah where my ancestors are buried so that I can rebuild it."

Then the king, with the queen sitting beside him, asked me, "How long will your journey take, and when will you get back?" It pleased the king to send me; so, I set a time.

I also said to him, "If it pleases the king, may I have letters to the governors of Trans-Euphrates, so that they will provide me safe-conduct until I arrive in Judah? And may I have a letter to Asaph, keeper of the royal park, so he will give me timber to make beams for the gates of the citadel by the temple and for the city wall and for the residence I will occupy?" And because the gracious hand of my God was on me, the king granted my requests. So I went to the governors of Trans-Euphrates and gave them the king's letters. The king had also sent army officers and cavalry with me.

When Sanballat the Horonite and Tobiah the Ammonite official heard about this, they were very much disturbed that someone had come to promote the welfare of the Israelites.

Preparation is Key

Nehemiah was planning for success, not failure ... even though he was afraid! He wasn't negative! He had not been idle from prayer time to request time ... he had a plan ready in the hopes that the king would be favorable to letting him speak!

Nehemiah had made plans and prepared specific requests for the king. *Having courage to do something for God does not mean just sitting back and waiting for God to let you know what to do.* That is very foolish. Nehemiah didn't just respond, *"Well, however the Lord leads me."* This may be a proper response if God has told you to wait on Him, but not in most cases! Note how the king questions Nehemiah about specifics and how quickly Nehemiah responds! He had thought of everything humanly possible ... he had made good plans.

When Nehemiah finds success, notice to whom he gives the credit. This is the ninth characteristic of courage: *acknowledging God in the process* and not patting yourself on the back (Chapter 2:8). The cupbearer is promoted to governor!

Nehemiah's success reveals the truth of the Word: Promotion to leadership comes best through servanthood!

Continuing Courage

It would have been a wonderful ending if Nehemiah's story had stopped here, but courage is not just for getting a new and frightening endeavor started. We don't find the way smooth sailing just because we're out of the planning stage.

Courage is needed for the whole process! Courage had only gotten Nehemiah past the first stage. Now, he would need a great deal more of it to finish the course God had called him to!

When you set out to do the will of God in your life, don't be shocked by the problems you continually stumble over. You need to hold on to your courage. Never, never quit.

Nehemiah runs up against two politically connected men who intend to battle him every step of the way! One is Sanballat – governor of Samaria – the chief rival to Nehemiah who was just appointed governor of Israel. Nehemiah and Sanballat are positioned to become true rivals!

Nehemiah's other rival, Tobiah, is a fellow Jew (or at least he believed in the God of Israel) ... and he would become a source of great opposition – from one of Nehemiah's own brethren!

The bottom line: If you are going to do anything for God, you are going to need courage! No one finds great rewards who doesn't display courage in times of great risk! The first stage of accomplishing the will of God in your life is taking the *courage* of God and *making it your own!*

The first step in accomplishing God's will for your life will be large doses of courage, so get prepared! Anyone who has ever accomplished great things for God has had to overcome their fears and move with courage.

It takes determination to do God's will!

PREPARATIONS

Nehemiah 2:11-15

I went to Jerusalem, and after staying there three days I set out during the night with a few others. I had not told anyone what my God had put in my heart to do for Jerusalem. There were no mounts with me except the one I was riding on.

By night I went out through the Valley Gate toward the Jackal Well and the Dung Gate, examining the walls of Jerusalem, which had been broken down, and its gates, which had been destroyed by fire. Then I moved on toward the Fountain Gate and the King's Pool, but there was not enough room for my mount to get through; so I went up the valley by night, examining the wall. Finally, I turned back and reentered through the Valley Gate.

Many Christians over-spiritualize ministry ... that is, they think that when God speaks, you simply jump into action and – *miraculously* – things happen! There are certainly times when this can be true, but if you look in the Bible, you will discover that most of the mighty works of God through His prophets and servants included a *significant preparation time* before their ministries were really effective.

Preparation for Service

How about Moses? He needed an extra 40 years of preparation in the desert!

Then there's Elisha who did a long apprenticeship under Elijah.

The apostle Paul had a dramatic revelation of the risen Christ on the road to Damascus, and God still required of him at least three years learning and submitting to the other apostles. Some commentators list an even longer time, including a 10-year silent period where after a few years Paul went back to his home territory. Only then was he called back by Barnabas, and they went off in ministry, with Paul under Barnabas' tutelage.

Samuel, the greatest prophet of Israel during the

time of the kings, spent his entire youth under Eli, the high priest, in preparation for his ministry.

The pinnacle of Biblical servants was Jesus, and He spent thirty years preparing for His three-year ministry. The Bible speaks of Him learning, submitting, and discussing the law in the temple at twelve years of age. Jesus *"grew in grace and knowledge."*

To simply leap into ministry without preparation is presumption. Only when God clearly indicates through the Word, sincere prayer, and consensus of the godly men and women around you that His will is for you to move immediately can you afford to jump into untested waters.

Careful preparations are a normal part of God's calling for ministry! Except under rare circumstances, we should expect to invest substantial time and resources to prepare ourselves for effective ministry. Failure to prepare for effective ministry is a failure to respond correctly to God's call for ministry, and this is true for all levels of ministry.

Arriving in Jerusalem

Nehemiah finally arrives in Jerusalem after a long journey and is anxious to start on the call of God. However, understanding the need for proper rest after a long trip, he wisely takes a few days off to recuperate.

Years ago, the concept of ministry was to go until you burned out for Jesus ... this was never good teaching! When you are exhausted and tired, you are not as tuned in as you should be ... creating the opportunity for poor judgment and mistakes.

In Ecclesiastes 3, Solomon says there is a "time for everything," including "work & rest"!

David talked about the importance of rest in Psalm 127:2:

In vain you rise early and stay up late, toiling
for food to eat – for he grants sleep to those
he loves.

The best servants of God needed proper rest and balance. Elijah, one of the great prophets of the Old Testament, was at a pinnacle of achievement after the victory with the prophets of Baal. Yet, God sent him on a forced rest. God gave Elijah a "leave of absence" to correct the balances in the prophet's life and bring him back into proper alignment with his life and with God.

Paul had to take a time of rest and instruction after his great revelation on the road to Damascus.

Balance is an important concept if you are going to be effective in God's work, whatever His call is upon your life! I'm constantly amazed by the number of people who can't seem to control their own schedules. Over the years, I've had many executives come to me and say with pride, "Boy, last year I worked so hard that I didn't take any vacations."

It's nothing to be proud of. I always feel like responding, "You mean to tell me that you can take responsibility for an $80 million project, and you can't plan two weeks out of the year to go off with your family and have some fun?"

What is interesting here is that Ezra did the same thing when he came to Jerusalem to rebuild the temple. "I assembled them at the canal that flows toward Ahava, and we camped there three days" (Ezra 8:15a). So did Nehemiah when he arrived to rebuild the crumbling walls! "I went to Jerusalem, and after staying there three days I set out during the night with a few others" (vv. 11-12).

When God's call involves circumstances that require no time for balance, He will miraculously provide the strength required. Most of the time, His call is more of a daily nature and thus the balances are left to good use of wisdom on our part!

Nehemiah 2:16-18a

The officials did not know where I had gone or what I was doing, because as yet I had said nothing to the Jews or the priests or nobles or officials or any others who would be doing the work.

Then I said to them, "You see the trouble we are in: Jerusalem lies in ruins, and its gates have been burned with fire. Come, let us rebuild the wall of Jerusalem, and we will no longer be in disgrace." I also told them about the gracious hand of my God on me and what the king had said to me.

Displaying Boldness

With freshness of spirit and body, Nehemiah displays boldness as he prepares for the time when they will build ... this included seeing the bigger picture! It is important in ministry to get the whole picture. *If you think only your ministry is important, you will be filled with pride. If you don't realize others are ministering also, you will be filled with despair ...* like Elijah, who thought he was the only prophet of God left! Nehemiah wanted to survey the city walls ...

get a realistic picture of what this call of God encompassed! Before diving into the job and asking others to dive into it with him, he knew he should be knowledgeable about the task ... as much as possible!

He realized he wouldn't be able to accomplish the ministry alone ... and felt responsible to know as much as possible before asking others to join in! With boldness (*and lots of rest beforehand*), he set out at night to get an honest picture of the damage.

We need to have a realistic picture of what encompasses a call from the Lord. Responsibility comes with the call ... a responsibility to do our homework. Nehemiah didn't put the job on someone else, either ... he took the responsibility to evaluate the situation on his own. This boldness was an example of *courage* – and he took a few good men along with him. He didn't have to preach or speak a lot, but he did have to show the way!

When it came to sharing the burden and the call, Nehemiah does not *confess* that things are better than they really are ... he tells it like it is! He needed to be honest about the real conditions ... and a full survey of the existing mess proved to be a real disaster. Things were really broken down ... the destruction was widespread! But to a man with a call from God, this wasn't discouraging ... just a better challenge! The greater the problem ... the greater the praise! Great risks ... *great rewards!!*

A Great Opportunity

Like David, when Israel only saw a *giant opposition* in Goliath, David saw a *giant opportunity*; they saw a *giant tyrant*, David saw a *giant target* – he couldn't miss! Be realistic ... then *be bold!* Nehemiah wasn't bothered by a huge task ... it would only make the reward that much more supernatural! There is nothing supernatural by itself in confessing away reality. That is little more than wishing. Confessing the reality of the situation and then believing God to give victory over it anyway is a supernatural leap into the glorious presence of our almighty God!

It was important for Nehemiah to first know the real extent of the job he had taken on and then to encourage his brethren with confidence and boldness to do the task! If he couldn't see the job as manageable, he could hardly expect to have the people believe that it was! Nehemiah first *prepares* himself before he *calls* on others to join him!

Booker T. Washington, in his autobiography *Up from Slavery*, tells of his older brother's kindness. The bristly, flax garments the slaves were given to wear irritated Booker's skin. His brother would wear Booker's new shirts to break them in and soften the fabric. It was an act of kindness the young Booker never forgot. Galatians 6:2 says we are to: "Carry each other's burdens, and in this way you will fulfill the law of Christ." Setting the example is an absolute for ministry ... those you minister to will not be so willing to serve if you are not willing to serve. If you are unfaithful, they will not be encouraged to be faithful to the task.

Nehemiah was ready; he had done his homework. He knew the damage, and he knew his God. As importantly, Nehemiah knew what was possible by faith and hard work!

Nehemiah 2:18b-20

They replied, "Let us start rebuilding." So, they began this good work.

But when Sanballat the Horonite, Tobiah the Ammonite official and Geshem the Arab heard about it, they mocked and ridiculed us. "What is this you are doing?" they asked. "Are you rebelling against the king?"

I answered them by saying, "The God of heaven

will give us success. We his servants will start
rebuilding, but as for you, you have no share in
Jerusalem or any claim or historic right to it."

Come, Let Us Build!

These people certainly knew the conditions of the wall. They had been living there without repairing them ... they had been complacent about repairs.

They didn't rebuild the walls because they lacked the courage and a burden to do so ... they just didn't see how it was possible!

This was where Nehemiah stepped into the picture. The people lacked badly needed leadership, someone who could help restore a sense of burden and faith to do the work! God was placing Nehemiah right where he was most needed!

It is very significant that Nehemiah gave them an honest appraisal of how bad the damage was ... lest they think him a fool or just a *"possibility thinker"* ... someone ignorant of the real truth. They learned that Nehemiah had done his homework. His honest appraisal of the conditions as they really existed told them that this man knew what they were facing!

Nehemiah didn't deny the enormity of the problem. If he had, they would have written him off as another outsider with fantasy solutions! His full and real description made them realize that here was a man who saw how big the task was ... and perhaps had a way to tackle it!

Notice that after his honest description of the problem, he also presents them with hope: "Come, let us build!" Here is a man who knew what leadership really meant ... he didn't say, "*You build* while I tell you what to do."

A New Level of Respect

Nehemiah offers himself as a fellow servant. His proposal inspires them, and they develop respect for his leadership! A title won't give you respect ... you earn that by being a servant!

He adds an important reason for rebuilding, too ... so that "we won't be in disgrace!" Jerusalem was the "City of Peace" ... God's chosen place for His people ... His temple was within the walls of the city, meaning His presence was among them in the city. It was a disgrace that God's dwelling place should be encompassed by brokenness. The brokenness – the tumble-down condition of the city and her walls – was not the core of the problem, only the symptom. It was the lack of concern about the brokenness that was the problem!

Their combined response was: "Let us start rebuilding!" All they needed was someone to lead the way.

The Real Work Begins

They needed a new look at an old problem. Nehemiah's leadership provided the boost they required. They were encouraged to believe the job was possible with God's help. If they were united — *even though they were small in number* — they could go ahead full steam!

If only the story had ended there, it would have been a happy ending. Everyone was excited. Their perspective had shifted from disinterest to seeing the job as a finished endeavor. They were anxious to get to work. They had shifted from *who cares* to *we care*.

Then the energy vampires, the soul suckers, and the emotional leeches gathered to drain the enthusiasm from Nehemiah and the work God had tasked him to do.

Isn't that like the world? Whenever we start to do good "works" for the Lord, we hear all the reasons it is not possible. People come out and begin to criticize us or the job we are doing.

Doing the works of the Lord is the evidence of our faith! James declares, "Show me your faith by your works" (James 2:18). There is nothing wrong about "works" in the Christian vocabulary ... it is certainly true that we are not saved *by* "good works," but we are saved *to do* good works! Real faith has real evidence! Only when real pressure has been applied can the strength of something be determined.

The real work wasn't rebuilding the fallen walls of Jerusalem. It was holding on to God's established promise that it would be done! The people were under pressure, and now they had to perform their "works" to prove their "faith."

The Detractors

Three men mocked the Jews for attempting to do the impossible: Sanballat the Horonite, Tobiah the Ammonite official, and Geshem the Arab!

At first, their sarcastic complaints attempt to turn the Jews' newfound enthusiasm into a big joke. They call out that they don't really believe the Jews can do it. They mock the people for being foolish and not facing up to reality. "What? A few people who managed to escape the exile and are still living in the area can rebuild these huge walls around the entire city? Do you really think you can do this?"

They even questioned their motives for rebuilding: "Ah, so you're planning a rebellion against the king?" Perhaps they thought that might put a scare into the locals!

At a point like this, it is important to hear from God ... which in this case meant through God's servant Nehemiah. This was not a time for Nehemiah to be silent. It was important for the people to see boldness and faith from their leader. It was also not a time to give way to a few complainers.

Nehemiah Takes Charge

Notice carefully how Nehemiah phrases his response. *"The God of heaven will give us success!"* If only some of the Jewish leaders of the past had remembered this point, the city walls might not have fallen in the first place! Our success comes from God ... but He expects our faithful service in the *process of success!*

Nehemiah also understands the people's role in the process of achieving their success. *"We his servants will start rebuilding ..."* And he carefully notes that those who do not participate will not have any of the shares of the blessing that is to come!

Some people are ready to jump on the bandwagon after the success is achieved, but they really don't appreciate the success like those who have built the bandwagon! Being involved in the process of God's work puts you in line to enjoy the fruit of His work.

After all, who doesn't want to be fruity? I know I do!

Nehemiah encourages the people with three facts:

1. These three troublemakers aren't even in the covenant family.
2. They have no historic right to discourage God's people from doing God's work.
3. If they listen to the outsiders, they will never get anything done for God – and this is still true!

The most effective ministry is accomplished by God's call and power ... combined with careful planning. To do God's good works, we must show patience. What God establishes is a step-by-step process that can take a significant amount of time! This kind of ministry produces long-lasting fruit!

Right Stuff

Nehemiah 3:1-5

Eliashib the high priest and his fellow priests went to work and rebuilt the Sheep Gate. They dedicated it and set its doors in place, building as far as the Tower of the Hundred, which they dedicated, and as far as the Tower of Hananel. The men of Jericho built the adjoining section, and Zakkur son of Imri built next to them.

The Fish Gate was rebuilt by the sons of Hassenaah. They laid its beams and put its doors and bolts and bars in place. Meremoth son of Uriah, the son of Hakkoz, repaired the next section. Next to him Meshullam son of Berekiah, the son of Meshezabel, made repairs, and next to him Zadok son of Baana also made repairs. The next section was repaired by the men of Tekoa, but their nobles

would not put their shoulders to the work
under their supervisors.

The government allocates huge sums of money for government programs. Why do so many of them fail? They often fail from lack of human commitment to the task or from an unmotivated bureaucracy.

It is like the dad who went outside to see what his sons were doing, and he found a group of neighborhood boys just meandering around quietly. He finally asked one of his sons what they were doing, and the boy replied, "We are playing war." The father was puzzled and asked why they were so quiet if they were playing war. "Because we are all generals, and we can't get anybody to do the fighting."

This is often the state of the church of Jesus Christ! We sing, "Onward Christian soldiers," but no one wants to dig in their heels and fight ... we are more like the crowd of people who watch war on TV and never get involved in the real war on sin!

It is time the saints of God quit watching church and start participating in church! This is no show ... there will be no commercials ... what we are doing is the most serious thing in the world right now! The church cannot succeed without volunteers and workers in the ranks!

The Word of God teaches us that if the church has the "right stuff," and by that I mean "workers," God can accomplish incredible feats that will astound the world ... and baffle the enemy! But it will take the whole effort by all the saints!

The Priesthood Takes the Reins

It is important to realize that the first to rally to the call to work were the high priest and the other priests.

They set the example as elders of the community.

They put themselves to the task joyfully! Not only do they rebuild the first section of the wall, but it was the section near the temple where they started, not near their homes!

They also dedicated their finished work as a sign of gratefulness to God!

The first gate repaired was the *sheep* gate opening to the pastures where the sheep were taken in and out of the city ... reflecting the nurture and need of the sheep which was so much a part and symbol of the people!

Elders then, as now, were held to higher standards. They must be the ones to set the pace of the Lord's work, and they must set their example willingly! Seeing the elders working, and not for their own benefit, must have been an encouragement to the people of God! Their leaders actually led! They weren't giving orders ... they were accomplishing God's orders together!

A Huge Task Ahead

There was a huge task facing the Jews in Jerusalem ... we are talking about rebuilding a wall and gates that were enormous in size and shape. To make this task even more difficult, only a scattered remnant of the Jewish people existed in Jerusalem at the time!

It was like asking a congregation of twenty people to buy land and plan on building a church that could seat over 1000! In the natural world, it would seem senseless – if it could be done at all!

God has never been bothered by small numbers ... if the people are ready to work! In God's economy, small numbers working together have great strength! It's known as synergism.

Picture this true story from Canada. You're at a horse-pull, and the crowd cheers when one horse pulls 9,000 pounds.

Then another comes up and pulls 8,000 pounds.

They team up the horses, not for 17,000 pounds, but to successfully pull 30,000 pounds. The mighty beasts can pull more as a team than they can pull alone. The simultaneous action of separate agents working together has a greater total effect than the sum of their individual efforts. More can be done in a team effort than can be accomplished alone.

For the principle of synergism to work, we must actively participate in *teamwork*. Everything we do takes teamwork and trust. Every person in the local church is valuable and needed. The church is a team, and together we can build for the Lord.

Refusing to Take Part

Verse five reveals an interesting attitude about the men from Tekoa, a small town about eleven miles from Jerusalem. These men could not get the "nobles" from their community to help.

"Nobles" here meant the "magnificent" ... men of wealth and power. They were unwilling to help their own brothers! Yet, they fully expected to be blessed by the protection that would later come from a strong Jerusalem once this wall was repaired!

Tekoa was the hometown of the prophet Amos. What would he have said about these insolent goof-offs?! The common folks from Tekoa, however, didn't become angry or bitter about the inaction of their mighty nobles, nor did they complain about having more to do with less help ... *they instead did another section of the wall* (v. 27) after finishing the one assigned them!

If God only gives you a few people with the right stuff, don't be discouraged. A few soldiers with God's help can overcome tremendous odds! The work of the kingdom must not be held up by all the correct things first having to be in place. Even when some won't serve, there are people ready to serve, no matter what!

This passage about Tekoa reminds me of a story about the missionary David Livingstone who worked alone − tirelessly − in Africa for many years. He received a message: "Is there a good road there? We have men who wish to join you."

Livingstone replied, "I only require their help if they don't require a good road."

Nehemiah 3:6-13

The Jeshanah Gate was repaired by Joiada son of Paseah and Meshullam son of Besodeiah. They laid its beams and put its doors with their bolts and bars in place. Next to them, repairs

*were made by men from Gibeon and Mizpah—
Melatiah of Gibeon and Jadon of Meronoth—
places under the authority of the governor of
Trans-Euphrates. Uzziel son of Harhaiah, one
of the goldsmiths, repaired the next section;
and Hananiah, one of the perfume-makers,
made repairs next to that. They restored
Jerusalem as far as the Broad Wall. Rephaiah
son of Hur, ruler of a half-district of Jerusalem,
repaired the next section. Adjoining this,
Jedaiah son of Harumaph made repairs
opposite his house, and Hattush son of
Hashabneiah made repairs next to him.
Malkijah son of Harim and Hasshub son of
Pahath-Moab repaired another section and
the Tower of the Ovens. Shallum son of
Hallohesh, ruler of a half-district of Jerusalem,
repaired the next section with the help of his
daughters.*

*The Valley Gate was repaired by Hanun and
the residents of Zanoah. They rebuilt it and put
its doors with their bolts and bars in place.
They also repaired a thousand cubits of the
wall as far as the Dung Gate.*

A New Type of Worker

A perfect example of synergism is the story of Gideon. At first, Gideon had 32,000 men to fight against an enemy of at least 135,000, according to Judges 8:10 ... yet not all these Jewish men were true warriors or willing to fight.

First, all the *faint-hearted* were asked to go – 22,000 men abandoned Gideon, leaving him with only 10,000 men. Second, God asks Gideon to have the *half-hearted* men leave – those who drank water without watching for a surprise attack – and another 9,700 men left. This left Gideon with 300 warriors ... but they were dedicated, conscientious, alert fighters!

This is the type of worker Nehemiah required, for a few dedicated men with a strong sense of commitment can get far more done than a huge crowd of half-hearted wannabes.

Nehemiah 3:14-21

The Dung Gate was repaired by Malkijah son of Rekab, ruler of the district of Beth Hakkerem. He rebuilt it and put its doors with their bolts and bars in place.

The Fountain Gate was repaired by Shallun son of Kol-Hozeh, ruler of the district of Mizpah. He rebuilt it, roofing it over and putting its doors and bolts and bars in place. He also repaired the wall of the Pool of Siloam, by the King's Garden, as far as the steps going down from the City of David. Beyond him, Nehemiah son of Azbuk, ruler of a half-district of Beth Zur, made repairs up to a point opposite the tombs of David, as far as the artificial pool and the House of the Heroes.

Next to him, the repairs were made by the Levites under Rehum son of Bani. Beside him, Hashabiah, ruler of half the district of Keilah, carried out repairs for his district. Next to him, the repairs were made by their fellow Levites under Binnui son of Henadad, ruler of the other half-district of Keilah. Next to him, Ezer son of Jeshua, ruler of Mizpah, repaired another section, from a point facing the ascent to the armory as far as the angle of the wall. Next to him, Baruch son of Zabbai zealously repaired another section, from the angle to the entrance of the house of Eliashib the high priest. Next to him, Meremoth son of Uriah,

*the son of Hakkoz, repaired another section,
from the entrance of Eliashib's house to the
end of it.*

The Tally of the Faithful

The list of names tells us that these were well-established men in Jerusalem ... they can be traced back to Ezra's ministry and the rebuilding of the temple under Ezra.

They remembered that being in the temple meant more than just prestige, it meant being a servant and working! They set the example as servants!

The next to take leadership and show an example were the well-established families within the family of God in Jerusalem. They understood the need to minister to the newer people by their example of being servants. They served as an example of willingness to work on a new project ... even though they had worked hard on the previous project of the temple years earlier!

The early sections built by the priests and other established men were the areas nearest to God's house ... demonstrating their realization that they were to serve God before self. Rather than first secure the walls near their homes, they focused on the more important matter and secured God's house.

Servanthood is an example in action, not just a concept.

Nehemiah 3:22-27

The repairs next to him were made by the priests from the surrounding region. Beyond them, Benjamin and Hasshub made repairs in front of their house; and next to them, Azariah son of Maaseiah, the son of Ananiah, made repairs beside his house. Next to him, Binnui son of Henadad repaired another section, from Azariah's house to the angle and the corner, and Palal son of Uzai worked opposite the angle and the tower projecting from the upper palace near the court of the guard. Next to him, Pedaiah son of Parosh and the temple servants living on the hill of Ophel made repairs up to a point opposite the Water Gate toward the east and the projecting tower. Next to them, the men of Tekoa repaired another section, from the great projecting tower to the wall of Ophel.

No Excuses Allowed

Undoubtedly, the nobles from Tekoa had their excuses: They were the merchants and kept supplies coming in, or they were busy with work. If they got hurt on the job, it might really upset their families. How could the government run without them? They already had everything they wanted ... so why do more? They weren't living in Jerusalem, so it wasn't their problem!

One might have said, "It probably isn't going to be finished anyway, so why waste all the time and effort?" Perhaps another one said, "We've lived this long without those walls, so why change things!?"

These are the same excuses people use today. Let's be honest ... we can always come up with an excuse if we really want to! In this case, other men did what they should have done. God doesn't just look at what we would *like* to do. His eyes are on what we *follow through with* once we've promised to do it!

Willing and Capable

What a wild combination of workers! So many kinds of tradesmen willing to build for God, completing tasks they were not trained to do! God can make anyone capable ... but they must be *willing* and *available!* Many of these people had never done this kind of ministry before, but with a willing heart, God enabled them to do it anyway! Don't say, "It can't be done" ... or "I'm not trained to do this." We can work on the training, but we need people to train!

The project was completed in 52 days! The walls had lain in ruins for almost 150 years, and a few people with the right stuff had them in proper shape again in only 52 days! We are talking about 4 miles of walls and gates! About 40 to 45 men were named as overseeing about 45 sections, and each section ran about 168 yards long, which meant they had to finish about 3-4 yards a day, allowing for Sabbath days off!

These walls were somewhere around 15 feet thick and around 25-30 feet tall!

Finding Our Motivation

What was their motivation? How could they bring such a big project to pass in such a short time? We find two reasons in the Word. Nehemiah tells us:

1. *They were empowered with the simple knowledge that God had brought all this to happen.* When you know a task is mandated by God, the gates of hell

cannot stand against you!

2. Their strength not only came from God but from the unity they had among themselves ... remember the variety of people who put themselves to the task!

God's will ... and man's willingness combined cannot be beat by the devil himself! What none of them could have done alone, they did together. Cooperation with a clear mandate from God's own Word got the job done!

The men working on the wall were like Old Testament Pentecostals. Look up the story of Azusa Street and the beginnings of the modern Pentecostal movement in 1906 through 1909. They worked *zealously.* They did *more than their share of the work.* We must be like the men of Tekoa, taking on more once they finished the first. Baruch ... stepped up and repaired *another* section.

Some people just aren't satisfied with doing only what they have to for God! We want to be like this man. He couldn't be stopped ... not until the job was done, and he inspired others!

Let me give you an example of how we can do more and go further in the church.

Sandhill cranes are large birds that traverse continents, traveling vast distances through all types of weather. How do they manage to travel so far?

Three reasons:

1. They allow different birds to shoulder the brunt of leadership. The same bird isn't always at the front of the formation as they force their way across the miles.

2. They pick a capable leader. Not all the birds can handle being out front. They must be able to handle the turbulence of the rising storm.

3. They cheer their leader on. We hear it as honking. It's affirmation to the leader that they are just behind, and they want to go farther and faster than before.

This is not a bad example for how our churches should be run. We should all be "honking our approval" of our church leaders. How can we do this? A pat on the back, a check in the offering, an invitation to lunch ... the ways are endless.

Nehemiah 3:28-32

Above the Horse Gate, the priests made repairs, each in front of his own house. Next to them, Zadok son of Immer made repairs opposite his house. Next to him, Shemaiah son of Shekaniah, the guard at the East Gate, made repairs. Next to him, Hananiah son of

Shelemiah, and Hanun, the sixth son of Zalaph,
repaired another section. Next to them,
Meshullam son of Berekiah made repairs
opposite his living quarters. Next to him,
Malkijah, one of the goldsmiths, made repairs
as far as the house of the temple servants and
the merchants, opposite the Inspection Gate,
and as far as the room above the corner; and
between the room above the corner and the
Sheep Gate the goldsmiths and merchants
made repairs.

Burn Out, Not Rust Out

Rest is vital for the workers of God. That's Biblical, but to do nothing while claiming we're "resting" is not what God intends! It is far better to burn out for God than it is to rust out! I like the family of Shallum (v. 12). It wasn't enough for this guy to do his share ... even his daughters helped!

Can you imagine the kind of enthusiasm that spread in the town with all these exciting saints working with all their hearts? They weren't counting the cost, just the privilege. They worked with a real sense of mission and with joy.

If they could do this big job then, can we do less

now? The willing servants in the book of Nehemiah who found the motivation to rebuild an entire city wall in less than two months can serve as encouragement to us, to show what can be done even when the task seems overwhelming ... if everyone will put their shoulders to the task.

We must remember that many have traveled this way before, so when the task God entrusts to us seems impossible, we must not be afraid to try. When we're doing nothing for God, our Christian witness is rusting away. Leave it too long, and soon it will be gone!

A Prayer for Our Time

If you're ever in Colorado, visit the Cave of the Winds near Colorado Springs. As you make your way up the sharp grade, the steep, winding road approaches a narrow section bordered by high rock walls. It seems impossible that a car could fit. Turn around, you think, but no! There's a sign that encourages you, saying, "Yes, you can! Millions of others have." You'll discover your car does, indeed, fit, and soon you are through to the wider road on the other side.

That's what God says to us. "Yes, you can complete the task I've given you. Get to it!"

Dear Father, you are our strength and our source of endurance to complete the task ahead. Show us the way, and let us not forget that "yes, we can, because millions of others already have." In Jesus' name. Amen.

God will make a way for us. He has proven His providence by doing it for others. (Read the Bible, Genesis through Revelation!)

God's Call

God has never called Christians to sit and be comfortable in church each week. *Each of us is a minister.* There is no such thing as laypeople! Too many church members want to be "lay" people ... sleeping all the time, letting others do the work!

We need ministers in the form of Sunday school teachers, nursery workers, Wednesday evening children's leaders. Our babies need them, our young children need them, the older children need them, the youth need them, and the unsaved need them. *God give us ministers!* It doesn't matter what your earthly occupation is ... in the church, God can use you in many ways. Find the spot or section of wall that you are supposed to work on, or the wall that will be left unfinished if you don't step up, letting the enemy slip in! Then get started!

It is amazing what can be done for God when ALL God's people get in on the action! Excitement breeds excitement, as examples encourage more examples! Nothing short of the miraculous happens when God's people pull together to build the work of God and to stand against the enemy of God and fight the odds! Are you working or wallowing!? Running or rusting? Giving God your all or waiting for someone else to step in and do it for you?

God's time is now!

BATTLING

DISCOURAGEMENT

Nehemiah 4:1-6

When Sanballat heard that we were rebuilding the wall, he became angry and was greatly incensed. He ridiculed the Jews, and in the presence of his associates and the army of Samaria, he said, "What are those feeble Jews doing? Will they restore their wall? Will they offer sacrifices? Will they finish in a day? Can they bring the stones back to life from those heaps of rubble—burned as they are?"

Tobiah the Ammonite, who was at his side, said, "What they are building—even a fox climbing up on it would break down their wall of stones!"

Hear us, our God, for we are despised. Turn their insults back on their own heads. Give them over as plunder in a land of captivity. Do not cover up their guilt or blot out their sins from your sight, for they have thrown insults in the face of the builders.

So we rebuilt the wall till all of it reached half its height, for the people worked with all their heart.

Satan has two effective weapons against Christians: fear and discouragement. Both wear down the saints and destroy the foundations of faith. The biggest battles you will face as a Christian are not the trials themselves ... but the discouragement and fear that trials can create in your heart. *A bunch of worn-down saints are little threat to Satan and yield little fruit for God!*

Weathered and Worn

Here are some of the things that can wear down the saints:

- A sense of insignificance ... feeling that you're nobody; or very unimportant.

- Apparent unfruitfulness ... with the emphasis on the word "apparent."
- Sustained temptations ... often wear down the saints of God.
- Human weakness ... a major factor, for everyone has a tiring or breaking point.
- Strife and discord in relationships ... can wear down saints.
- Suffocating pressures of personal needs ... can breed discouragement and then fear ... this leads then to a lack of faith.

This is where the Jews rebuilding the walls of the city under Nehemiah's tutelage found themselves. Battered by men who ridiculed their progress, many of them must have felt weathered and worn as they labored to complete the task.

Constant good deeds and staying on top can wear down even the strongest saints! This is what happens sometimes with faithful ministers who suddenly crash.

Fighting Discouragement

Every saint of God will face discouragement more than once in their lifetime. So, how do you fight discouragement? Nehemiah reveals important steps that must be taken to fight against discouragement.

A starting point is focus. We must keep our eyes on God and not on us or our circumstances. God's Word teaches us that we are not helpless in discouragement. There are Biblical steps we can take that will help us fight against discouragement and the negative traits that discouragement ultimately brings into our hearts.

Ignore the distractors. Discouragement starts with jealous but vocal opposition. Sanballat feels threatened and jealous and becomes quite angry. His reaction to the Jews' and Nehemiah's plans was to ridicule them. Ridicule is often an effective method of creating discouragement! This is a tactic of Satan's that you will face frequently. Sometimes this even comes from your own brothers and sisters in Christ – or worse ... *from yourself!*

Be your own chief fan. If you ridicule yourself, don't be surprised if you get discouraged! Notice however that Sanballat doesn't ridicule alone ... he does this with an entourage of other threatened and negative people. Critics and jealous people tend to hang together. This gives them a greater sense of right and power when they are negative. Sanballet's associates were present and so was the army of Samaria. As Christians involved with the work of the Lord, we must step aside from those who are outside God's plan and cheer ourselves on to do the good work of the Lord!

Nehemiah's Prayer

Notice the use of their distractors' intimidating language: "*These feeble Jews*." Discouragement, then intimidation, now backed by heavy sarcasm, and finally ... *exaggeration* are all effective weapons for creating discouragement.

The onslaught of all this discouragement makes an impact ... it creates a reaction alright. Notice Nehemiah's prayer:

> *"Hear us, O our God, for we are despised. Turn their insults back on their own heads. Give them over as plunder in a land of captivity. Do not cover up their guilt or blot out their sins from your sight, for they have thrown insults in the face of the builders."*

This prayer is similar to many of the imprecatory psalms that David and others wrote invoking judgment or calamity in moments of honest anger against their enemies!

But there are some good points to how Nehemiah chose to respond that we can learn from in this prayer:

FIRST: He prays instead of trying to argue with his enemies! It is useless to argue against discouragers! It is better to run to encouragement ... *God!*

SECOND: He is honest in the prayer about how they all are feeling ... *despised!*

THIRD: He prays for God to really do them in!

Before getting too upset about this, Nehemiah is simply venting toward God rather than outwardly toward his enemies, thus keeping himself under control, the whole point of an imprecatory prayer. Nehemiah's prayer may seem harsh at first glance ... but it also reflects an important attitude in Nehemiah that helps to deflect discouragement: *"God, You are in control and ultimately all enemies of God will get theirs!"*

The point is to get perspective and not to create a pattern. Nehemiah's prayer assumes that if they don't change, he hopes for justice! At least his prayer is honest ... and the anger is *not* directed at the enemy in an open way ... he confines his anger to an appropriate place ... *prayer!*

Nehemiah 4:7-12

But when Sanballat, Tobiah, the Arabs, the Ammonites and the people of Ashdod heard that the repairs to Jerusalem's walls had gone ahead and that the gaps were being closed, they were very angry. They all plotted together to come and fight against Jerusalem and stir up trouble against it. But we prayed to our God and posted a guard day and night to meet this threat.

Meanwhile, the people in Judah said, "The strength of the laborers is giving out, and there is so much rubble that we cannot rebuild the wall."

Also our enemies said, "Before they know it or see us, we will be right there among them and will kill them and put an end to the work."

Then the Jews who lived near them came and told us ten times over, "Wherever you turn, they will attack us."

Finding Realistic Goals

With his anger properly directed and his perspective properly focused, Nehemiah now can deal with the discouragement which has been lifted through these healthy outlets.

Notice verse 6: "So we rebuilt the wall till all of it reached half its height." This is important for fighting discouragement: Instead of building sections all the way up while others are barely started, he works on all the parts to come together into a full and complete circle, even if only halfway up!

This brings a sense of completion and a realization that the work can be done, a very practical and balanced approach to try and build confidence against discouragement!

Finding realistic goals is important in fighting discouragement. If you're fighting discouragement, it's better to reach a lower goal. Keep going by accomplishing part of the task rather than getting overwhelmed and quitting before doing anything! In essence, Nehemiah ignored the discouragers ... but also carefully planned some realistic goals to help the people see real accomplishments ... and thus be encouraged!

Afraid of Their Own Shadow

There's a story about Alexander the Great that illustrates this perfectly. At sixteen, the young Alexander went with his father to see whether a horse was suitable for purchase. The animal was unmanageable, jumping away from its own shadow.

Alexander, showing signs of his future greatness, turned the animal's head toward the sun, mounted it, and got it under control.

Millions today are "afraid of their own shadow," the "shadow" of their evil deeds, the haunting "shadow" of their own guilty conscience and the "shadow" of hundreds of fears and failures. But let some faithful Christian point them to Christ, and their shadows immediately fall behind them, for Christ is "the Light of the world" (John 8:12), and all who follow Him "shall not walk in darkness, but shall have the light of life." The closer one walks to Christ, the more light he has; and the farther one gets from Christ, the deeper the shadows. And he who is so foolish as to walk away from Christ in unbelief, that person walks ever deeper into the shadows that will eventually plunge him into the eternal darkness.

Nehemiah 4:13-15

Therefore I stationed some of the people behind the lowest points of the wall at the exposed places, posting them by families, with their swords, spears and bows. After I looked things over, I stood up and said to the nobles, the officials and the rest of the people, "Don't be afraid of them. Remember the Lord, who is great and awesome, and fight for your families, your sons and your daughters, your wives and your homes."

When our enemies heard that we were aware of their plot and that God had frustrated it, we all returned to the wall, each to our own work.

Serious Practical Steps

The point: *Encouragement requires some serious practical steps to ward off discouragement!* Don't just sit around after praying and wait for God to zap you with encouragement! When Nehemiah's enemies realized they had failed at discouraging the saints of God through ridicule and sarcasm, they tried another tactic ... *fear*. More negative people are added to the already negative crowd ... and they plot together a terrorism strategy... surprise attacks! If Satan's work of ridicule and mocking doesn't stop us, he will step to another tactic, that of fear! Once a good dose of fear sets in, little worry of ministry results!

There are 365 "fear nots" in the Bible – one for each day. Courage is not the absence of fear; it is the mastery of it.

Nehemiah's Response

Nehemiah's response to this new threat of fear was two-pronged: *First*, go to God! He starts with praying to God. *Second*, he takes practical steps to deal with the real fears! The genuine threat here was that a surprise attack would occur and demoralize the people from further work ... so guards were posted at the most likely places of attack! I can't emphasize enough how important *both steps are* here!

Some Christians are good about going to God but don't take any practical steps to negate the real fear of what the world can bring against us. God will step in to accomplish what we can't – including protecting us against the enemy – but He expects us to do what we *can* do!

The people of Israel, goaded into action by Nehemiah, didn't just pray. They also posted a guard *day and night.* They did what they could. Prayer is not a shortcut to success. Our effort is required, also.

The people's response showed a healthy balance in dealing with fears. Going to God first, then using their heads to do what they could do to minimize the fears! If we do the first and never the second, we will remain in fear! If we do the second and not the first, we will never have the peace of God that He will be handling the parts that we can't deal with! The balance is found in both!

Tired and Drained

The enemy was making an impact, however. Despite their determination and Nehemiah's encouragement, the people were getting tired. Perhaps at this point, they were worn out by the backbreaking work in completing the project, and now they had to play army as well! This project was turning into more work than they originally thought ... they hadn't planned for playing the role of guards as well as building!

This is something we all face when life becomes more than we bargained for. Tiredness overwhelms us at the height of our enthusiasm. Exhaustion drains our resolve to work, which only slows down our work and gives proof to the belief that this is too much for us!

The historical giant Martin Luther was known to become depressed. As the story goes, one day his wife appeared dressed in black. When Martin Luther questioned her, surprised, she said that God had died, and she was in mourning.

"What?!? God died? Never!" Martin Luther exclaimed.

"Then live and act like He is alive!"

The tiredness had allowed fear to take hold ... as they repeated the plans of the so-called surprise attack! The result of this fear: *trembling!* Verse 12 tells us that their own brethren told them *ten times over:* "Wherever you turn, they will attack us!"

Nehemiah 4:16-23

From that day on, half of my men did the work, while the other half were equipped with spears, shields, bows and armor. The officers posted themselves behind all the people of Judah who were building the wall. Those who carried materials did their work with one hand and held a weapon in the other, and each of the builders wore his sword at his side as he worked. But the man who sounded the trumpet stayed with me.

Then I said to the nobles, the officials and the rest of the people, "The work is extensive and spread out, and we are widely separated from each other along the wall. Wherever you hear the sound of the trumpet, join us there. Our God will fight for us!"

So we continued the work with half the men holding spears, from the first light of dawn till the stars came out. At that time I also said to the people, "Have every man and his helper stay inside Jerusalem at night, so they can serve us as guards by night and as workers by day." Neither I nor my brothers nor my men nor the guards with me took off our clothes; each had his weapon, even when he went for water.

We Can Do It

Nehemiah quickly steps in lest the whole project collapses! He doesn't start yelling at the people or calling them lazy. He doesn't criticize them or complain about them ... this would have only driven the discouragement deeper! He comes up with a plan that is both practical and involves everyone ... and deals with the worst-case possibility!

Nehemiah's masterstroke strategy also communicates confidence: We can do it ... together with God's help!

FIRST, Nehemiah *leaks to the enemy the message* of how God helped them to know about the surprise attack, thereby taking away from the enemy their sense of power over them ... and he gives the credit to God! Now, Nehemiah is demoralizing the enemy ... the enemy must have wondered how the plans were leaked to the Jews ... in other words, someone or several of their own people had warned the Jews about the surprise attack. They must have traitors in their camp! This turn of events gave the Jews new courage ... and new motivation!

SECOND ... just in case, Nehemiah *plans for the attack!* He equips the people for battle in an organized fashion. We see a similar plan for our families in Ephesians 6. We will run into snags in life (just as the work on the city's walls had run into several snags) but that is always the case when you do something for God. You can't be shaken by the unexpected, just deal with it as it comes! Organizing is key! Establish a plan that's fair to everyone and *get on with it!*

A New Opportunity

Have you heard the story of Harlan Sanders, the founder of Kentucky Fried Chicken? He retired from the post office, received his first retirement check, and said, "This can't be the end." He started his restaurant chain, retired a second time from leadership of the enterprise, and began his third career as a public relations representative for the company.

Discouragement can become a steppingstone to greatness. Nehemiah didn't lose heart with all the unplanned interruptions. He could have said, "Look, God, when I agreed to do this, I didn't think it also included etc. etc. etc." He dealt with each problem that arose *as* it arose and kept the vision in sight! He also affirmed his faith in God as a priority with each obstacle that arose! He came up with unique solutions that were fair and practical!

Teamwork Makes the Difference

It is significant that Nehemiah *trusted* in God first but also called the people to *work and fight as a team!* Teamwork can lessen the impact of fear and discouragement. The whole team is not impacted equally at the same point of weakness, enabling those who are in a position of strength to encourage those who are struggling.

In Nehemiah's case, the nobles and the common men were treated equally. They were to consider everyone as their equal and come and fight if they needed help!

They would need each other ... not just Nehemiah, but each other! Nehemiah couldn't possibly meet all their needs, but as a whole they could minister collectively to all their individual needs!

Nehemiah had built a *spiritual wall* of teamwork and cooperation around the Jews long before they finished the physical wall around Jerusalem! Only teamwork would result in the wall being complete ... and in such a short time.

Anything done for God will face conflicts. Conflicts can be demoralizing — or they can be a time of dynamic growth. Fighting discouragement successfully is a two-fold process:

1. Trust in God's power!

2. Give total, genuine participation on your part!

Our success in achieving God's goals through trust and participation gives revival and victory over discouragement and fears!

The Inside Enemy

Nehemiah 5:1-11

Now the men and their wives raised a great outcry against their fellow Jews. Some were saying, "We and our sons and daughters are numerous; in order for us to eat and stay alive, we must get grain."

Others were saying, "We are mortgaging our fields, our vineyards and our homes to get grain during the famine."

Still others were saying, "We have had to borrow money to pay the king's tax on our fields and vineyards. Although we are of the same flesh and blood as our fellow Jews and though our children are as good as theirs, yet we have to subject our sons and daughters to slavery. Some of our daughters have already been enslaved, but we are powerless, because our fields and our vineyards belong to others."

When I heard their outcry and these charges, I was very angry. I pondered them in my mind and then accused the nobles and officials. I told them, "You are charging your own people interest!" So, I called together a large meeting to deal with them and said: "As far as possible, we have bought back our fellow Jews who were sold to the Gentiles. Now you are selling your own people, only for them to be sold back to us!" They kept quiet, because they could find nothing to say.

So I continued, "What you are doing is not right. Shouldn't you walk in the fear of our God to avoid the reproach of our Gentile enemies? I and my brothers and my men are also lending the people money and grain. But let us stop charging interest! Give back to them immediately their fields, vineyards, olive groves and houses, and also the interest you are charging them—one percent of the money, grain, new wine and olive oil."

Nehemiah and the people were halfway to their goal. They had successfully fought off the outside enemies and their attempts to derail the goal God had given them to build, and those that had threatened them were already fading as a danger.

Now, without the threat from external forces, a new and potentially worse enemy was rising to threaten them ... this enemy really could destroy the work of God in their midst.

Who was this great enemy? *Tiredness and selfishness ... inside the camp!*

Fighting the Inside Battle

While outside enemies tend to cause the saints of God to rally together against a mutual threat, these inside enemies tend to do just the opposite. They divide the people of God and turn brother against brother and sister against sister!

It's like hummingbirds around a feeder. We supply the feeder and keep it filled with the sweet nectar, yet when several birds approach the feeder, there is always a high-ranking bird that will drive the others off. It doesn't matter the number of openings available. The lead bird will claim them all.

How often do Christians fight over God's gifts, when we've done nothing to earn them? We grow weary in the work God gives us to do, and selfishness emerges. Eventually, people walk away, and the work of God is left unfinished!

We need true repentance and everyone working for the shared goal! The Word of God teaches us that *we all* are called to minister in the kingdom of God ... that our mission is one that is shared by *all*, and that Satan's most effective weapon against the church is turning brother against brother.

We see this happening to the Jews under Nehemiah. They came brother against brother, laying foundation to a very serious potential problem. Several wealthy Jews had loaned money to other Jews at high interest rates, even taking their children as pledges for further loans! The rich Jews refused to participate in rebuilding the city walls, feeling they were too powerful to get down on hands and knees and work like the rest of Israel.

Instead, they saw a way of getting rich off the sacrifices of the others during the process. Instead of giving, they had found ways of taking ... and they were *taking everything* from those giving sacrificially!

Proof of Their Selfishness

Their attitude of "I don't have to help unless there is something in it for me" demonstrated their selfishness. It wasn't just a matter of laziness; they robbed their own people unfairly!

There is no excuse for this kind of behavior in the kingdom of God. Selfishness is highly destructive to the body of Christ, for it goes against the very nature of God and is in fact the endemic nature of sin! Their attitude of "I don't want to help, but I do want to benefit from the sacrifice of others" was about to undermine the entire project and society of Israel! While Sanballat and the army of Samaria and the other leaders in the area who were against Israel couldn't stop the project or take away the joy of the people, this inside selfishness and ungodly behavior by a few poised a very serious threat to the entire success of the community!

"We Are Powerless . . ." (v. 5)

Note the sense of helplessness in these words! This is the cry of the victims of selfishness. This is the hopelessness of all sinners. Sin holds us in a grip that cannot be broken without Jesus Christ.

The people had no way of helping themselves. Without help from an outside source, all would soon be lost because of a few selfish and uncooperative brethren!

Hopelessness becomes the norm when selfishness takes over ... there is nothing more draining than trying to deal with a selfish person ... no matter what you say, they turn it around to their advantage! It is a heart problem ... a *sin problem!* The actual root and nature of sin *is selfishness!*

You've heard of the cuckoo bird. It never builds its own nest. The cuckoo finds another bird's nest and lays its egg to be hatched by the adoptive parents.

Here's the thing, though. When the cuckoo hatches, it begins to force the other babies from the nest. One by one they are pushed out, until only the cuckoo remains.

The parents continue to feed the cuckoo until it outgrows the nest, the parents, and all the food they can provide.

Here's our lesson: What we feed grows until it consumes everything around it. If we feed our selfish nature, it will overtake our spirit. If we feed our spiritual nature, selfishness will be pushed aside, and our spirit will thrive.

The wealthy Jews around Jerusalem were feeding their carnal, selfish nature, and the hardworking Jews were being pushed from the nest of God's righteousness and the plan they had committed to complete.

Nehemiah's Anger

There is a sense of powerlessness when trying to deal with a selfish person! What could they do ... they had nothing left to bargain with or to buy food with! A few people held the entire community hostage to their own selfishness and cold hearts! While the majority had given freely, a few had taken so much that the rest of the community was in despair.

Nehemiah steps onto the scene once he discovers the reason the people are crying ... and the actual charges against the corrupt brothers. A holy anger grips Nehemiah's heart when he discovers the rotten situation, and he sets an example on how to deal with such selfish individuals!

It became necessary to call off the work and get the whole community together!

Some issues cannot be ignored, or they can poison the whole endeavor! God's work – rebuilding the walls of the city – was in jeopardy of not being completed because of a few lazy, selfish individuals whose motives were to get rich at the expense of the whole group! It was time for a Word from God!

Mastering Our Emotions

Nehemiah recognized that if the correction came from his anger, they would use him as an excuse to dismiss their guilt and continue their selfish activities.

Mastering our emotions – *especially as leaders in the church* – is a sign of genuine maturity, a quality that is necessary in leaders! Nehemiah was able to master his own feelings or "separate them" from the situation to be as objective as possible in dealing with the problem.

Nehemiah wanted to be sure the wrongdoers were confronted with the real and complete details of their ways. He wanted them to bear their own guilt. He didn't want them to use the excuse of his out-of-control emotions to dismiss their responsibility! His example is one for us to follow still!

The Shoes of a Prophet

So, Nehemiah steps into the shoes of a prophet and proclaims the error of the profiteers! He is clearly in control as he presents the evidence, ensuring that those being accused will have a chance to speak in response to the charges.

When he is finished, the evidence is *so clear* that they choose not to try and defend themselves ... their guilt was obvious! Their selfishness and lack of help was an *open-and-shut case!* This exhortation from Nehemiah was *what was needed* to prevent the community of the saints from dissolving into a divided body of people!

Nehemiah continues to explain just how damaging these selfish individuals were! He explains how their selfish needs and wants impacted the witness of the whole community before the ungodly nations around them! They would soon become a laughingstock to the other Gentile nations! Their enemies would mock God ... by seeing that they had destroyed themselves without outside help!

Nehemiah explains how being fair in business was acceptable, but to take advantage of their own brothers while they worked hard to benefit the whole nation was the worst of motives!

Nehemiah says that the only solution for this problem was *immediate* repentance ... *to be fair and not selfish* ... to confess their selfishness and poor motives and return the unfair appropriations! Nehemiah could ask them to do this since he himself had practiced this very thing! This is an important aspect to being able to minister this correction; he was practicing what he was preaching!

Nehemiah 5:12-19

"We will give it back," they said. "And we will not demand anything more from them. We will do as you say."

Then I summoned the priests and made the nobles and officials take an oath to do what they had promised. I also shook out the folds of my robe and said, "In this way may God shake out of their house and possessions anyone who does not keep this promise. So, may such a person be shaken out and emptied!"

At this the whole assembly said, "Amen," and praised the Lord. And the people did as they had promised.

Moreover, from the twentieth year of King Artaxerxes, when I was appointed to be their governor in the land of Judah, until his thirty-second year—twelve years—neither I nor my brothers ate the food allotted to the governor. But the earlier governors—those preceding me—placed a heavy burden on the people and took forty shekels of silver from them in addition to food and wine. Their assistants also lorded it over the people. But out of reverence for God I did not act like that. Instead, I devoted myself to the work on this wall. All my men were assembled there for the work; we did not acquire any land.

Furthermore, a hundred and fifty Jews and officials ate at my table, as well as those who came to us from the surrounding nations. Each day one ox, six choice sheep and some poultry were prepared for me, and every ten days an abundant supply of wine of all kinds. In spite of all this, I never demanded the food allotted to the governor, because the demands were heavy on these people.

Remember me with favor, my God, for all I have done for these people.

Genuine Repentance

The response seemed genuine and earnest: "We will give it back," they said, "and we will not demand anything more from them. We will do as you say."

Genuine repentance is reflected here ... which means they acknowledged their guilt and restored what they had taken wrongfully. There can be no forgiveness for sins if they are not acknowledged as sin! Repentance occurs only when we admit our guilt before God! True repentance leads to restoration whenever possible.

Nehemiah understood that confession with the mouth is good ... but that there must be action or evidence to back up genuine repentance! So, the priests were called in to create an oath that they would accept as *proof* of what they said was genuine sorrow! Action must follow confession of the mouth ... evidence of change is necessary when real forgiveness is accepted!

Cheap grace is the deadly enemy of our church. Cheap grace means grace sold on the market like cheapjack's wares. Cheap grace is the preaching of forgiveness without requiring repentance, without church discipline, communion without confession, and absolution without personal confession.

The evidence Nehemiah required of the repentant Jews included entering into a spiritual contract with God that would demonstrate itself by a change of actions!

The forgiven sinner is a changed saint! Your actions demonstrate your heart!

The Moral High Ground

Nehemiah, therefore, sets the tone of the moral high ground expected of leaders and God's people.

- Fairness.
- Leading by example ... and not by lording over them.
- Demonstrating an unselfish lifestyle by not taking even what he could have as governor. In fact, instead of receiving what was rightfully his, he gave it back by sharing it with others; he was not a taker but a giver!

Nehemiah's closing words in this chapter reveal the two reasons he was involved with the people in the first place:

1. Reverence for God.
2. Love for God's people.

In this way, Nehemiah really fulfilled the Law of Christ: "Love the Lord your God with all your heart and with all your soul and with all your mind and with all your strength" (Mark 12:30, NIV) and "Love your neighbor as yourself" (Mark 12:31, NIV). Selfishness is not becoming as a saint of God; it is a characteristic of our worst enemy! Nehemiah understood how a little sin in the camp can rob God's people of the joy of serving Him.

Everyone was needed to minister if the walls were going to get finished on time ... their greatest threat wasn't from the outside ... but from within!

Nehemiah's overall goal can be found in Nehemiah 5:19: "Remember me with favor, O my God, for all I have done for these people." The favor of God! Not earthly rewards! He asks nothing from the people except the opportunity to serve.

As the Jews discovered, when our enemies are beaten, there is an even greater danger to the body of Christ ... division within! While most of the Jews worked to rebuild the walls, a few took advantage of the majority. They were motivated by selfish gain, and they robbed the joy from the hearts of the workers. Only genuine repentance restored the joy and fellowship of God's people.

The surrounding enemies hadn't stopped the people of God, but the enemy within could! Churches are rarely destroyed from outside forces ... they are more likely to succumb to poor motives, selfishness, and disunity!

We are one people in the Lord. Let's keep our bonds strong and continue building for the kingdom of Christ!

Promises and Pitfalls of Detours

Nehemiah 6:1-4

When word came to Sanballat, Tobiah, Geshem the Arab and the rest of our enemies that I had rebuilt the wall and not a gap was left in it—though up to that time I had not set the doors in the gates— Sanballat and Geshem sent me this message: "Come, let us meet together in one of the villages on the plain of Ono."

But they were scheming to harm me; so I sent messengers to them with this reply: "I am carrying on a great project and cannot go down. Why should the work stop while I leave it and go down to you?" Four times they sent me the same message, and each time I gave them the same answer.

Detours. They promise new scenery, a better direction, even improved fortunes.

Many Christians are waylaid by them – only to discover they are worse off than before! Then, they fall back on excuses or logic to put the blame somewhere besides where it belongs.

The way of the world is a detour on the way to God and the truth of the Word. It is better to not see or experience Satan's detours. The consequences can be painful and long-lasting!

Satan's Detour

If Satan can't get you to detour, he will settle for tricking you into slowing down. "You need more rest, more time for yourself. It is time for others to do their share, etc."

That's all the detour that Satan needs, a little slow-down to keep you from doing God's work. While you do need rest at times, and others should step up and do their part, these excuses can also be a sly trick of Satan to slow you up enough that your ministry is zapped of its momentum! We need to discern the difference so that we can avoid the devil's whispers of, "There is no burry. There is no hurry."

Staying on Course for God

The Word of God teaches us to stay on course and avoid the spiritual detours that seem to offer so much. They give nothing but pain. We must be careful to know the difference when God is asking us to step up ... or when Satan is attempting to slow us down. We need to be able to recognize God's voice, whether it comes through the reading of the Word, the ministry of the pulpit, or a word of direction from a Christian saint. It can make *all the difference* in our ability to achieve our spiritual goals in ministry!

Ask Jonah how much fun a detour can be! Most Christians have stumbled at one time or another as they learned to walk closer to God. Nehemiah and the people of God were about ready to finish the walls ... just hang the gates in place and the vision will be complete ... mission accomplished! Then the enemy leaped up and tried a cunning detour to prevent this completion of the wall!

A Desperate Distraction

Nehemiah's enemies asked for a meeting with

Nehemiah in a place that was an equal distance for all of them to travel ... about a day's journey away. Four times he gets this message to meet ... and four times he refuses.

Nehemiah knew his enemy, and they weren't interested in his well-being. When the devil tries to distract us in our walk for God, we must be able to recognize him. We must say, "This is the devil's work. I recognize the pattern of his distraction and misleading temptation. NO!!"

We must be like a child that, no matter how poor, we prefer the love of our parents over the riches that glitter in the windows of the houses of the rich. Partaking of the treats Satan dangles before us is no consolation for the love of our Father in heaven.

And understand, Satan can be quite persistent, hoping we will wear down and give in! Nehemiah was in no mood to believe his enemy wished him well, and we should never think the devil wishes us well! As often as Nehemiah's enemies tried to wear him down by repeated invitations, he simply and politely refused. He was doing a *great work for God* ... it was already in motion and nearly completed ... why take off now and lose momentum?

Nehemiah 6:5-10

Then, the fifth time, Sanballat sent his aide to me with the same message, and in his hand was an unsealed letter in which was written:

"It is reported among the nations—and Geshem says it is true—that you and the Jews are plotting to revolt, and therefore you are building the wall. Moreover, according to these reports you are about to become their king and have even appointed prophets to make this proclamation about you in Jerusalem: 'There is a king in Judah!' Now this report will get back to the king; so, come, let us meet together."

I sent him this reply: "Nothing like what you are saying is happening; you are just making it up out of your head."

They were all trying to frighten us, thinking, "Their hands will get too weak for the work, and it will not be completed."

But I prayed, "Now strengthen my hands."

One day I went to the house of Shemaiah son of Delaiah, the son of Mehetabel, who was shut in at his home. He said, "Let us meet in the house of God, inside the temple, and let us close the temple doors, because men are coming to kill you—by night they are coming to kill you."

The Stakes Are Raised

When the repeated invitations failed, the enemy tried something just a little more persuasive ... an *open letter!* You may say, "So what?"

Think about it ... an *open letter* would allow the carrier to know the contents. He would tell his best friend ... and his friend, and so on, and so on, etc., until it became a widespread rumor!!!

It was brilliant! It was devious! It might even work! But that was the point ... the enemy is slick! We can never afford to underestimate the enemy. We must be looking through God's eyes, measuring every circumstance against the Word of God, and evaluating our responses through our prayers and the advice of our church elders.

The open letter contained an accusation that Nehemiah was planning on secretly becoming king when the walls and gates were finished. The letter claimed that Nehemiah would turn against the very King who had granted him the privilege of rebuilding Jerusalem's walls!

Emotional Blackmail

This sort of behavior was common in Nehemiah's day. The accusation seemed entirely plausible ... creating just what the enemy was counting on – *emotional blackmail!* The idea was to ruin Nehemiah's good reputation and force him to withdraw to King Artaxerxes to answer to the king about the letter's contents ... and to forestall the work of God!

Of course, the letter included the "reasonable and kind" offer by the enemy to meet with him to "talk this matter over" ... making it appear that the enemy wished to help! Satan often plays these games with people. He appears as an angel of light, making the detours alluring, and he even sounds logical and concerned, with our best interests at heart! ... *But don't be fooled!*

Nehemiah 6:11-16

But I said, "Should a man like me run away? Or should someone like me go into the temple to save his life? I will not go!" I realized that God had not sent him, but that he had prophesied against me because Tobiah and

Sanballat had hired him. He had been hired to intimidate me so that I would commit a sin by doing this, and then they would give me a bad name to discredit me.

Remember Tobiah and Sanballat, my God, because of what they have done; remember also the prophet Noadiah and how she and the rest of the prophets have been trying to intimidate me. So the wall was completed on the twenty-fifth of Elul, in fifty-two days.

When all our enemies heard about this, all the surrounding nations were afraid and lost their self-confidence, because they realized that this work had been done with the help of our God.

Nehemiah Finds Confidence

Nehemiah doesn't allow his feelings to interfere with what he knows are God's plans. He isn't taken in easily ... *why? Because he is confident that the king knows the real Nehemiah* ... and his good reputation is stronger than this false rumor! It is important to realize that his *established* good reputation was now his *trump card!*

Nehemiah was not blind to what the enemy was trying to do ... *discourage* him and the people and disrupt the building of the wall! His second solution was *prayer!* It was a simple prayer but effective! The temptation to quit was real (v. 9) ... But this was the time to revive and not quit. When Satan raises the bar and tries to make our lives difficult, we can rest assured he fears our ministry being effective!

A Near Misstep

Nehemiah visited the local priest. Why, we can't be for certain. Prophets and priests of the day were known to do strange things to communicate God's Word, and the priest was sequestered in his house by his own will. Likely, Nehemiah was curious, seeing this as a possible message from God.

Shemaiah, the priest, seemed genuinely concerned about Nehemiah's life and ministry and tells him about a plot of the enemy to have him killed — possibly that very night. It seemed the Lord was using Shemaiah to warn Nehemiah about a real threat! Of course, if Nehemiah ran and hid, he would be out of action for a while ... the same result as if he returned to King Artaxerxes to deal with the accusations in the letter. The project God had given them to complete would be shut down, exactly as his enemies wished!

Everything about the warning seemed authentic and very real. After all, this was God's servant speaking. *Except* – one thing didn't fit ... and Nehemiah would not have caught the enemy's cunning trick if he hadn't known the Word of God! The Word clearly forbids any access into the temple's holy areas for anyone except priests (Numbers 3:10, 38; 18:7; and Deuteronomy 18:20). If anyone other than a priest enters, he is to be put to death! Following the priest's advice would violate God's Word. Nehemiah was not a priest. For Nehemiah to go into the holy area to hide ... Why would God ask him to violate His own Word?

Jesus said of the Pharisees of His day: "They be blind leaders of the blind. And if the blind lead the blind, both shall fall into the ditch" (Matthew 15:14). We need to be very careful not to entrust our souls to the guidance of someone who cannot see the clear teachings of our Lord, Jesus Christ. Our eternal destiny is too important to put at such risk.

For the priest to have suggested this, knowing it was wrong ... it must have been that the enemy had paid him to do this thing.

Nehemiah's Triumph

Nehemiah triumphed because he knew the Word of God. His knowledge protected him from a very clever trick of Satan's that at first seemed caring and real! Jesus encountered this kind of temptation three times in Matthew 4:1-11. Each time Satan used partial Scriptures ... and Jesus beat Him because He knew the Word better than the devil! *We need to know God's Word in this day and age of false prophets and ministries that appeal to the flesh!* Nehemiah exposes all the false prophets in town! Instead of Nehemiah getting a bad name ... all the false prophets in town were exposed by God's Word, and they lost their reputations and ministry! When you run with the devil you will fall with him ... join his cause and you will join his collapse!

"So the wall was completed ... in 52 days!" The miraculous happened because there were no side trips or detours! Israel's 40 years in the wilderness should have only been a couple of months, but they took a detour that cost them 39+ years of wandering around! Nehemiah's stubborn insistence to keep to God's call and continually ignore the enemy allowed the great project to not only be completed on time, but it testified to the enemy that *truly God was with them!* What a testimony for Nehemiah, too! If he had fallen prey to the enemy's subtle plots of distraction

and disaster, the people who looked to his leadership would have floundered! Nehemiah realized that if he held steady, those who looked to him for guidance would fall into step behind him and follow his lead.

Give us *God-fearing* leaders!

Give us *people who will not stop* just because the enemy offers attractive alternatives and detours!

Nehemiah 6:17-19

Also, in those days the nobles of Judah were sending many letters to Tobiah, and replies from Tobiah kept coming to them. For many in Judah were under oath to him, since he was son-in-law to Shekaniah son of Arah, and his son Jehohanan had married the daughter of Meshullam son of Berekiah. Moreover, they kept reporting to me his good deeds and then telling him what I said. And Tobiah sent letters to intimidate me.

A Lesson for Sanctification

As a final word in this part of the story, we see more *stubborn willfulness!* Tobiah (the enemy) had a son who had remarried into an influential family inside Jerusalem ... a daughter of God's people *mar-*

ried to a man from the enemy! Nehemiah was forced to repeatedly defend himself because of this improper marriage. As he ends this wonderful success story about completing the wall, he reminds us of the intimidation the world can throw at us when we refuse to sever every connection with our past life of selfishness and sin! Tobiah continues to harass Nehemiah because of this marriage. Nehemiah refuses to allow this to rob the people or himself of the proper expression and appreciation of having done the will of God despite the enemies' constant barrage of sabotage ... but that's another sermon, next week!

Let's face it, there will be troublemakers in the Kingdom ... somehow they get connected ... but you can't run around constantly trying to put out small fires. You just keep moving forward in God and keep your eye on the bigger picture. Focus on the saints who desire God's will and are willing to work to see things happen! Troublemakers slot neatly into Jesus' words about the poor, *"These you will always have with you ..."* (Matthew 26:11).

Reaching the Goal

Just as Nehemiah and God's people were about to reach their goal, the enemy offered some tempting detours. When Nehemiah refused to take these detours, the enemy tried to catch him in devastating traps. By staying on course ... and drawing on a healthy knowledge of God's Word, they reached the goal, and the enemy sulked in weakness and defeat!

What are some of Satan's detours that affect us today?

- Unresolved anger
- Jealousy
- Bitterness
- Gossip
- Lies
- Lust
- Envy
- Rebellious attitudes
- Material cravings that are never met
- Self-pity
- Sexual values contrary to Scripture, etc.

Have you drifted off course or fallen into Satan's detours? Get back on track and you'll make the goal!

WE NEED ORDER IN GOD'S COURT

Nehemiah 7:1-5

After the wall had been rebuilt and I had set the doors in place, the gatekeepers, the musicians and the Levites were appointed. I put in charge of Jerusalem my brother Hanani, along with Hananiah the commander of the citadel, because he was a man of integrity and feared God more than most people do. I said to them, "The gates of Jerusalem are not to be opened until the sun is hot. While the gatekeepers are still on duty, have them shut the doors and bar them. Also appoint residents of Jerusalem as guards, some at their posts and some near their own houses."

Now the city was large and spacious, but there

were few people in it, and the houses had not
yet been rebuilt. So my God put it into my
heart to assemble the nobles, the officials and
the common people for registration by
families. I found the genealogical record of
those who had been the first to return. This is
what I found written there:

A great deal of effort had gone into building the city of God, the temple first and then the massive walls around the city. The people had really put their shoulders to the task for both jobs and now a firm city was established ... but one important thing was yet missing!

While they had built the city of God, they hadn't reflected on the need to build the citizenship of the city of God! While they could rightly rejoice over the city being ready ... they needed to reflect on the citizenship being ready to begin again as the people of God, displaying a special calling and unique life-style. They needed to find each other and become one again with joy before God.

And so, as the people prepared to rejoice over the finished product of the city, Nehemiah took the initiative to reestablish the proper order of the people themselves and their unique calling as the people of

God! ... *Then rejoicing would be full!*

Order Out of Chaos

All healthy life forms must have order to fulfill their purpose and impact the world. Using Biblical illustrations, the church is the body of Christ, Jesus the head, and the Holy Spirit is the energizing agent. It is vital for the body (the church) to have structure and order to be coordinated and united in function. God has ordained order for the health of the church ... and to ensure the greatest expression of rejoicing!

Change was in the air in ancient Jerusalem. With the city walls completed, it was time to turn to the concerns of the worshipping community.

Holy Ground

The priests and Levites comprised a large segment of the population of Jerusalem, as indicated by the census; it only seemed good to use these men at the gates of the city ... since they were accustomed to being gatekeepers at the house of God. This would add uniqueness to the city not experienced before. Now, along with the regular guards posted at the gates, there would now also be the spiritual guards ...

and since the central function of Jerusalem was worship, it would be quite fitting!

Think of entering this city of God, and as you approach the gates, you hear songs of praise coming from the singers and Levites stationed at the gates ... you are literally greeted to town by songs of praise! Think how this would affect your mindset as you entered town. You would become aware that you had entered "*holy ground*." You were joining in with the "people of God" in the "city of God!"

Protecting the City

These gatekeepers were to watch over the coming and going of the people, ensuring protection to God's special people. In this sense, they acted like *pastors*. It was their duty to be sure no thieves entered to rob the people. They were to keep the enemy from escaping (should one sneak in). They made sure the sheep gate was opened and closed properly to allow for the sheep to enter and leave at appropriate times ... under guard!

Here's a note to consider for our modern churches. The gates of the city were likely opened each day with songs of praise ... and shut each day with songs of praise. We should try it today. What a great way to start and stop the day!

Ensuring Good Leadership

Nehemiah also appointed two special men to work together in overseeing the congregation of God. His brother Hanani was put in charge of Jerusalem itself ... it is interesting to note that this was how Nehemiah first learned of Jerusalem's fate and need (see 1:2-4) ... thus he knew who had the greatest burden for the people of the city!

Nehemiah knew that leadership involves a heavy burden ... not just the prestige of being in control at the top! His brother had a great burden for the people and had proved to be a great servant, even to the point of submitting to his brother's leadership when Nehemiah came and took over the project. He who could serve well in second place would do well serving at the top!

Nehemiah made one other appointment, this one for the army of God's people. Hananiah was appointed commander of the citadel ... the great fortress that was next to the temple to protect the city and temple from the north. This man was chosen *first* because of his integrity and respect for God, and *second* for his military prowess. His reputation was impeccable. He loved and respected God more than most other men. His life reflected an obvious devotion to God that outshone the rest. He would be someone who would lay down his life for the sheep if necessary. This is the call of the pastor.

Extra Precautions

Important precautions were taken to account for the way the enemy worked to ensure the greatest safety of God's people.

The gates were only to be open in the light of day. The enemy likes to sneak in during darkness ... but there would be no way in since entrance was *only in the light!* This is still the only way into the kingdom of God. Jesus is the Light of the World, and you can't sneak into the kingdom of God without approaching through this light! Membership requires salvation ... becoming part of the people of God!

An enemy trying to get in during daylight while men were sitting at each gate singing the praises of God would really be intimidated! The people could go about their daily tasks rejoicing in the peace of Jerusalem which came by godly men looking out for them and the city. Jerusalem could really live up to its name ... the City of Peace!

These extra precautions ensured that not just anybody could creep into the city and upset the fellowship and unity of God's people. These measures helped prevent the disunity that might come from those whose hearts were not really with the people of God! It was necessary to have these extra precautions to prevent pollution from outside sources! It didn't mean a closed society ... the gates were open, but coming in meant being bombarded by singers and light at the entrance and holiness and godly living within. The whole community was in unity in the name of God! The only way to be comfortable in a place like this was to become a worshipper! Those who only pretended were miserable!

Nehemiah 7:6-63

These are the people of the province who came up from the captivity of the exiles whom Nebuchadnezzar king of Babylon had taken captive (they returned to Jerusalem and Judah, each to his own town, in company with Zerubbabel, Joshua, Nehemiah, Azariah, Raamiah, Nahamani, Mordecai, Bilshan, Mispereth, Bigvai, Nehum and Baanah):

The list [included] the men of Israel ... the

*priests ... the Levites ... the musicians ... the
gatekeepers ... the temple servants ... the
descendants of the servants of Solomon ...*

*[Many from] the towns of Tel Melah, Tel
Harsha, Kerub, Addon and Immer ... could not
show that their families were descended from
Israel:*

New People Needed

The city was huge and mostly empty. Few people
were enjoying all this tranquility, joy, and unity! The
people's priority had been their relationship to God
and rebuilding the city of God. They had not yet
rebuilt their own homes ... now they could begin.

Yet, there weren't enough people to fill the homes
that were there. Many of their people remained in
exile and captivity. The only solution ... *fill the town
with new people as well as getting back those who
rightly belonged there!* God put in Nehemiah's heart
a mandate to search for the people who belonged in
the city ... those who were truly the people of God!

They were going on an evangelistic tour!

First, Nehemiah checked the good standing of
those within the city, making sure they were really the
people of the covenant of the promise made to Abra-

ham! Others would be welcomed, but they would have to wait until there would again be a priest with the *urim and thummin*.

Today, we're no longer sure exactly what these devices were, but we know their purpose. Urim means yes and thummin means no. These were devices to reveal God's direction. Records had been lost during the diaspora of God's people. The *urim and thummin* would reveal whether those without proof of their ancestry could claim their place in Jerusalem's society.

The point is this: *There were plenty of places for more people! This can always be said about the church ... We want you ... More can come ... We'll find places for you; the kingdom of God is not crowded by any means!* Come into the light through the true gate called Jesus and join the people of God as we live and celebrate our life in Christ together! Enjoy the peace and security of knowing that others of like faith are looking out for you ... as you join in praises to our King of Kings! *It is a great place to live out your life ... not just a great place to visit!*

Nehemiah 7:64-69

These searched for their family records, but

they could not find them and so were excluded from the priesthood as unclean. The governor, therefore, ordered them not to eat any of the most sacred food until there should be a priest ministering with the Urim and Thummim.

The whole company numbered 42,360, besides their 7,337 male and female slaves; and they also had 245 male and female singers. There were 736 horses, 245 mules, 435 camels and 6,720 donkeys.

Sorting the Records

Nehemiah calls up the membership list to check on the present inhabitants. He needed to see proof they counted as part of the body of saints in the holy city. At that time, only those whose records could be traced to Abraham could be declared "pure" or as able to serve within the body of believers ... this was part of the covenant of promise with Abraham.

Yet, others had gotten in, joining the children of Israel's roll of respected members. Gentiles like Ruth, Rahab, and others were allowed in *when they embraced the God of Abraham and willingly aligned their lives with God's people*, thus rejecting their old ties to the world and false idol worship.

Once these Gentiles came in the proper way, they too were included in the records of God's people! As Nehemiah went down the roll call, most went well except a small group of people who had no records connecting them to God's family ... even some priests were missing their records tying them to God's family. They were not allowed to serve in positions of authority until the matter could be worked out ... but this was not as hard as it sounds! They were not being rejected completely, only until a high priest could consult God using the urim and thummim. For these it meant waiting ... but there was hope ... God does not reject those who hearts yearn for Him and whose faith is established in Him!

The point of all this was to make sure the people were pure ... that these really were the declared people of God ... and that the leadership was drawn from the rolls of those who were sons of Abraham ... according to the law of Moses!

A Holy People

Today, we need to be sons of the living God ... sons and daughters of God Himself through Jesus Christ according to the law of Christ who gave Himself up for all those who believe in Him! God wants a holy people and a pure people who will be able to do great things for Him as they are united in spirit and in purpose! Proper citizenship was a crucial issue to the health and stability of Israel's life and call as God's people … and it still is in the church today! Sloppy citizenship would not establish the holy city of God, nor will it a church body today.

Celebration Ensues

Notice what breaks out once the leaders of the city are established by godly means! Generosity breaks out … by the leaders first and then by the people! Where there is joy … there is kindness and inclusion! When God's people are united … peace becomes the rule in the church. There is a celebration of Christ's life that seeks to reach out and give to others!

Show me a joyful saint, and I will show you a generous saint. By the same measure, show me a generous saint and I will show you a joyful one! Joyful saints like to give out from themselves in service and in other ways! Rarely do you have to motivate a happy saint … steering them is more the issue! It is interesting that here and in other places in the Bible we see recorded the actual giving records of the people

... God does take notice of the many ways we give, and the amounts!

This abundant joy supplied abundant necessities and extra above what was required ... the result was that the temple of God and the needs of the people were well taken care of ... they would *all* enjoy the fruits of holiness and unity!

Nehemiah 7:70-73

Some of the heads of the families contributed to the work. The governor gave to the treasury 1,000 darics of gold, 50 bowls and 530 garments for priests. Some of the heads of the families gave to the treasury for the work 20,000 darics of gold and 2,200 minas of silver. The total given by the rest of the people was 20,000 darics of gold, 2,000 minas of silver and 67 garments for priests.

The priests, the Levites, the gatekeepers, the musicians and the temple servants, along with certain of the people and the rest of the Israelites, settled in their own towns.

Linked in Fellowship and Service

Now they could all go to their respected homes, not to be separate, but linked together as partners. They would share their goods and even share their townspeople. Many towns sent a tenth of their citizens to live in Jerusalem to help populate the city ... the city would thus become the common link for all the cities in Israel ... they would be linked together *by the holy fellowship of God's people serving in the holy city in God's presence!*

So, although many returned to their individual towns, because of the people sent from each town to live in Jerusalem, the country was *linked by the fellowship of the chosen people of God!* Finally, they could settle down in harmony and peace, and security and praise could be the norm again.

Those who had been scattered because of their previous sins were now being brought together to live in the land in peace again! The enemy had a new respect and fear of God's people ... the rebuilt walls of Jerusalem and the unity of the Jews had proclaimed the power of God and the strength of God's people. They refused to compromise or quit!

An Example of Community

God would once again make His people an exam-

ple of what the community of God could be like ...
filled with *peace, security, joyful celebration, fellowship, contentment, and praise*. In truth, these are the
natural byproducts of a well-ordered fellowship when
it is established with clear godly leadership and clear
directions for adding new members.

The next encounter we will have with Jerusalem
will be a great revival ... they were ripe for a great
move of God in their presence now that they were
properly established within the walls of the city.

Through unity and doing things God's way, the
people of God reached incredible milestones and
achieved incredible power. God establishes His
people when they purpose to follow His ways and His
plans.

TIME TO REJOICE

Nehemiah 8:1-3

All the people came together as one in the square before the Water Gate. They told Ezra the teacher of the Law to bring out the Book of the Law of Moses, which the Lord had commanded for Israel.

So on the first day of the seventh month Ezra the priest brought the Law before the assembly, which was made up of men and women and all who were able to understand. He read it aloud from daybreak till noon as he faced the square before the Water Gate in the presence of the men, women and others who could understand. And all the people listened attentively to the Book of the Law.

It is unhealthy for an individual to never be happy

or joyful ... God never intended for us as Christians to be miserable or always filled with guilt. Some people really struggle with their relationship to God because they can never seem to feel good about how God feels about them!

Worshipping in the Word

In verse 2, the people requested Ezra to come to them in the public square and read the Word of God to them and teach them! Can you imagine people begging to have the pastor get together with them for more preaching?

The assembly was not just the men ... it was the women and children, as well! This could not have taken place in the temple due to restrictions of who could enter; it was held in the public meeting place in town! This makes it unusual as well ... they wanted God's Word proclaimed from the center of the city for all the citizens to hear!

Here's the amazing part: Ezra read the Word of God for six hours straight! As amazing, the people listened for all six hours of the message! Not only that, but they all stood for the entire time ... without complaining of length or heat, or boredom or hunger!

The final interesting or unusual feature comes in

the last line of verse 3: "And all the people listened *attentively* to the Book of the Law."

Attentively is the key word here. They didn't just attend because everyone else was. They didn't bring something else to occupy their time when they got bored. They were soaking it all in for the entire six hours ... while standing!

They were hungry for spiritual things. When God tells them to celebrate, at first they begin to cry, a sure sign of their devotion in the worship of the Lord.

Blended in Unity

It is a worthy thing to note that they assembled together as *one* man! The concept is similar to the book of Acts when they were all together in *"one accord."* When God's people are blended in unity, there is almost a guarantee that God's Spirit will move in a great way ... look at the day of Pentecost!

In Psalm 133, David says that "It is beautiful when brethren dwell together in unity, like precious oil ... there God commands His blessing, even life for evermore!" Worship should be a time of both brokenness *and* great joy ... not just a time of mourning!

When we gather today to worship, it should be with a sense of joy and anticipation ... Paul said to the

Philippians, "Whatever is good, pure, joyful ... of good report, to think on these things!" There is nothing sad about being related to God through His Son Jesus Christ!! We are all equals in the church. We are brethren coming together in unity!

Nehemiah 8:4-9

Ezra the teacher of the Law stood on a high wooden platform built for the occasion. Beside him on his right stood Mattithiah, Shema, Anaiah, Uriah, Hilkiah and Maaseiah; and on his left were Pedaiah, Mishael, Malkijah, Hashum, Hashbaddanah, Zechariah and Meshullam.

Ezra opened the book. All the people could see him because he was standing above them; and as he opened it, the people all stood up. Ezra praised the Lord, the great God; and all the people lifted their hands and responded, "Amen! Amen!" Then they bowed down and worshiped the Lord with their faces to the ground.

The Levites—Jeshua, Bani, Sherebiah, Jamin, Akkub, Shabbethai, Hodiah, Maaseiah, Kelita,

Azariah, Jozabad, Hanan and Pelaiah—
instructed the people in the Law while the
people were standing there. They read from
the Book of the Law of God, making it clear
and giving the meaning so that the people
understood what was being read.

Then Nehemiah the governor, Ezra the priest
and teacher of the Law, and the Levites who
were instructing the people said to them all,
"This day is holy to the Lord your God. Do not
mourn or weep." For all the people had been
weeping as they listened to the words of the
Law.

No Condemnation in Christ

When frustrated Christians hear a message about forgiveness, they immediately respond by thinking, "Yes, I need to confess more," instead of hearing how wonderful it is that God has forgiven and forgotten their sins!

They forget that the word *gospel* itself means "Good News," or verses like: "There is therefore *now no condemnation to those in Christ* ..." or "All things are possible ..." or "We are more than conquerors ..."

In Romans 8:37, the Greek word is "υπερνικομεν," or "hupernikomen," meaning, *super conquerors!*

They also forget that "All things work together for good to those who love the Lord" or "God so loved ..." or "Who shall separate us from God's love ... nothing shall!"

A Joyless Life

Some believers never believe anything good! They live out their life in Christ in fear and discouragement, and because they are so down on themselves, they often are down about other Christians, as well. Misery loves company, as the old saying goes!

This joyless life kills all sense of motivation, so fruitfulness turns into fruitiness and fruitlessness. These joyless Christians are miserable when other believers are happy! They feel cheated; but they have really cheated themselves!

God desires His people to know *His joy!* Joy is the very strength of our faith. Our fruitfulness comes from having God's joy in our lives as a character trait! This is why God's Word declares that it is the "Joy of the Lord that is our strength!" Also, "A merry heart doeth good like a medicine."

Nehemiah 8:10-12

Nehemiah said, "Go and enjoy choice food and sweet drinks, and send some to those who have nothing prepared. This day is holy to our Lord. Do not grieve, for the joy of the Lord is your strength."

The Levites calmed all the people, saying, "Be still, for this is a holy day. Do not grieve."

Then all the people went away to eat and drink, to send portions of food and to celebrate with great joy, because they now understood the words that had been made known to them.

A Desire for More of God

The people preparing for Ezra's reading were so enthused that they built a large wooden platform for the occasion. The Hebrew wording for this text suggests this event was not planned by the religious leaders, but by a spontaneous desire by the people to learn more of God's Word. The people had anticipated a large gathering and so built the platform to enable the priest to be above the crowd so he could be seen and heard easier – they didn't want to miss a thing! This is where our concept of a platform in church buildings comes from. And for the same reason ... to elevate the pastor's voice (not his ego).

Notice in verse 4 that Ezra's associates were on the platform with him ... to give support and be examples of leaders for the people.

Here are the five core nuggets to take from this:

1. This was an unprecedented event ... the planning of it was by the people.
2. The construction was by the people.
3. The desire was of the people.
4. The hunger for the Word was from all the people: men, women, and children!
5. This is really where revival comes from ... a hungry congregation!

They stood for six hours as the Word of God was read! Notice Ezra's response to this sight: *"He praised the great God!"* And suddenly all the people *"lifted their hands and responded. Amen! Amen!"* (In Hebrew, a repeated word meant special emphasis!) This service was going places, Ezra was vibrant with joy ... and the people followed by joyous shouts of *praise* and agreement (the meaning of the word amen).

Nehemiah 8:13-15

On the second day of the month, the heads of all the families, along with the priests and the Levites, gathered around Ezra the teacher to give attention to the words of the Law. They found written in the Law, which the Lord had commanded through Moses, that the Israelites were to live in temporary shelters during the festival of the seventh month and that they should proclaim this word and spread it throughout their towns and in Jerusalem: "Go out into the hill country and bring back branches from olive and wild olive trees, and from myrtles, palms and shade trees, to make temporary shelters"—as it is written.

Passion for Worship

From praise, they entered into worship ... as they all bowed down and worshipped God as a group! Imagine the unbelievable sight of this ... especially for Old Testament times, rarely had such a hunger like this existed in the people of Israel. At other times, they had gone through long periods where their worship was little more than ritual ... and uneventful! In the past, it had often been religious practice but without passion. We don't need more religion; we need more *passion* in our relationship with God, a healthy passion, the kind that is balanced!

Here's where the balance part comes in: Passion alone often leads to emotionalism.

What brings the balance? The Word and the desire to understand it! The Levites walked among the congregation during Ezra's reading of the Word and explained to all those who desired the understanding of the text. They explained what the Word meant and how God desired their response. They moved among the people *"making it clear and giving the meaning so the people could understand what was being read!"*

We still do this today! This is the point of preaching, to teach the meaning of God's Word and suggest ways the lessons can be applied to our lives and lifestyle today. Preachers who only tell you what the text says but not what it means to you haven't finished their job. We don't need sermons that simply inform us just how bad the world is. We need sermons that also tell us what we can do to make it a godlier place! Preaching is not just a conclusion to a time of worship ... it is the focal point of where our worship is going ... to God ... then God speaks to us from His Word. A worship service is a two-way conversation and fellowship with a real and mighty God!

Do Not Mourn

There should be a fitting conclusion time to a service as well. Here, the people respond to their new understanding of the Law of Moses by weeping, probably because they became aware of their failure to live up to God's Word in the past.

It is awesome to understand who God is. The people listening to Ezra didn't get it, yet. They were stuck in the past with their failures! They were filled with sorrow for what they hadn't done and forgot to celebrate what God was doing for and through them right then. Their reaction to the Word of God was because of their *past* failures as a people of God!

We need to realize that the past is over, and we are no longer who we were in the past. We are exiles who have returned to God and are now children of the King.

The Jews were exiles in return. They had rebuilt the temple and the city walls! They had changed but didn't fully realize who they were *now*. They saw their old failures and began to weep, but Ezra saw who they were *now* and immediately jumped in to correct their response!

His instruction is simple and to the point: "*Do not mourn or weep!*" Their focus was wrong ... they were looking at the *old* Israel ... They were the new and renewed Israel! It was not a time to focus on failure or past mistakes but to rejoice in their revitalized faith. They were now God's people!

Nehemiah 8:16-18

So the people went out and brought back branches and built themselves temporary shelters on their own roofs, in their courtyards, in the courts of the house of God and in the square by the Water Gate and the one by the Gate of Ephraim. The whole company that had returned from exile built temporary shelters and lived in them. From the days of Joshua son of Nun until that day, the Israelites had not celebrated it like this. And their joy was very great.

Day after day, from the first day to the last, Ezra read from the Book of the Law of God. They celebrated the festival for seven days, and on the eighth day, in accordance with the regulation, there was an assembly.

A Time to Rejoice

Nehemiah instructed them how to respond to the six hours of instruction. They had just finished dealing with the consequences of their old sins. They had rebuilt the city walls. It was not a time to mourn the past but to celebrate the new. The people needed to rediscover how to express joy. They had been through many months of hard labor, and the enemy had come at them from all sides. Threats from the enemy camp had nearly been their downfall.

Certainly, there was a proper time for tears and sorrow; that time was during their captivity. But there comes a time when we need to move beyond sorrow, when our sins are already forgiven, and we are new creatures in Christ. It's time to celebrate our new life and realize that the *"joy of the Lord is our strength."*

To continue to stew in sorrow after our sins are forgiven is to mock the cleansing power of Christ and to put ourselves into false bondage once more. Don't do it. Rejoice in the freedom that comes from having our sins forgiven!

Finally, the Jews understood Nehemiah and took his instructions to heart, and did they ever celebrate! They ended up doing a double festival, one right after the other! *Boy, did they feel strong!*

Applying Nehemiah's Lesson to Today

Some Christians could learn from this. They are always so mournful over their past that they never feel good about themselves as Christians ... they never really appreciate who they *are now* in Christ ... they are still mourning and feeling burnt out by Satan, who likes to remind them of their past errors and what a failure they are (What they once were would be more accurate!).

There is no strength in unhealthy mourning! If you have committed your past sins to Christ for forgiveness, then *for heaven's sake, forgive yourself and get on with some joy as a cleansed saint*, not a condemned *sinner!*

It can be unhealthy to be joyful all the time (Wait until chapter 9 when they do have some things to cry about!), *but it is also unhealthy to never be joyful* as a saint of God. Miserable Christians are not much of an attraction to the faith. They will not lead many to Christ unless they find someone who loves being miserable, too! And the new convert will be weak as a Christian ... unable to cope with life and struggling with minor issues that others joyfully cast aside or overcome! Sorrowful saints find that motivation is next to zero, so they never do anything that gives them joy. Then they are angry at others who are happy and can do everything!

Ezra told the people to *get together* and celebrate ... not go off alone and find their own happy spot. Christians having some joyful times together *with other Christians* can be a great buffer against pining and self-pity! Make sure you pick joyful Christians to fellowship with ... they have obviously learned to appreciate their relationship with God and can help you with yours!

A Universal Truth

What is the universal truth for us in this passage? That it is possible to lose the joy and passion of worship and our relationship with God if we forget the meaning of the gospel and the *meaning of our practices!* Why does it state in verse 17 that "... the Israelites had not celebrated like this since the days of Joshua, son of Nun"?

In Joshua's day, God's victory was celebrated with great joy because it was new, the meaning fresh ... and the victory great since they were in the Promised Land ... they had left the past mistakes back in the wilderness!

What it means here is that they had rediscovered the fresh meaning of an old celebratory ritual!

We can fall into the same ruts of worship, too ... forgetting the meaning of what and why we are here! When this happens, tiredness and boredom set in, and there is a great loss of joy. The purpose of being together as a church gets lost over petty issues and sidetracked minds! The final verse says it all ... "Day after day, from first to last they ... celebrated." It even went on for 8 days! We should have such a problem with worship!

Like the writer of Ecclesiastes stated, "There is a time to cry, and a time to laugh." Just make sure there is a time for both, or you'll become a very *bitter saint* instead of a *better saint!*

Real revival always comes from a spiritual hunger to understand God's Word. When God fills this hunger, we find ourselves flooded with fresh joy, and through this joy, we discover fresh strength! If you know Jesus ... and desire to know His Word, then look out. He will pour out His joy, and the church will celebrate!

HUMILITY

Nehemiah 9:1-5a

On the twenty-fourth day of the same month, the Israelites gathered together, fasting and wearing sackcloth and putting dust on their heads. Those of Israelite descent had separated themselves from all foreigners. They stood in their places and confessed their sins and the sins of their ancestors. They stood where they were and read from the Book of the Law of the Lord their God for a quarter of the day, and spent another quarter in confession and in worshiping the Lord their God. Standing on the stairs of the Levites were Jeshua, Bani, Kadmiel, Shebaniah, Bunni, Sherebiah, Bani and Kenani. They cried out with loud voices to the Lord their God. And the Levites—Jeshua, Kadmiel, Bani, Hashabneiah, Sherebiah, Hodiah, Shebaniah

and Pethahiah—said: "Stand up and praise
the Lord your God, who is from everlasting to
everlasting."

One of the greatest statements in the Bible is by Jonathan, the son of King Saul. In 1 Samuel 23:17, he says to David (who had been his father's enemy, but not Jonathan's enemy): "I will be second to you." The rarest man in the orchestra of God is the saint who knows how to play second fiddle well!

It is the humble man who can recognize who God really is and who he himself really is! Instead of being discontent all the time, the humble man recognizes God's leading and is content wherever he is led ... even if it means being second fiddle!

Humility is healthy but sometimes painful. Humility is an honest appraisal of the past but with one difference. Instead of mourning over the past, it remembers so the past is not repeated! Humility sears our heart with sorrow over our past deeds, with the intent to heal the present and give wisdom and direction for the future!

Humility is meant to play an active, healthy role in our lives ... it should not end in self-pity. That is not true humility but humiliation! Real humility is solution-oriented in a healthy direction!

Nehemiah 9:5b-18

"Blessed be your glorious name, and may it be exalted above all blessing and praise. You alone are the Lord. You made the heavens, even the highest heavens, and all their starry host, the earth and all that is on it, the seas and all that is in them. You give life to everything, and the multitudes of heaven worship you.

"You are the Lord God, who chose Abram and brought him out of Ur of the Chaldeans and named him Abraham. You found his heart faithful to you, and you made a covenant with him to give to his descendants the land of the Canaanites, Hittites, Amorites, Perizzites, Jebusites and Girgashites. You have kept your promise because you are righteous.

"You saw the suffering of our ancestors in Egypt; you heard their cry at the Red Sea. You sent signs and wonders against Pharaoh, against all his officials and all the people of his land, for you knew how arrogantly the Egyptians treated them. You made a name for yourself, which remains to this day. You divided the sea before them, so that they passed through it on dry ground, but you hurled their pursuers into the depths, like a stone into mighty waters. By day you led them with a pillar of cloud, and by night with a pillar of fire to give them light on the way they were to take.

"You came down on Mount Sinai; you spoke to them from heaven. You gave them regulations and laws that are just and right, and decrees and commands that are good. You made known to them your holy Sabbath and gave them commands, decrees and laws through your servant Moses. In their hunger you gave them bread from heaven and in their thirst you brought them water from the rock; you told them to go in and take possession of the land you had sworn with uplifted hand to give them.

"But they, our ancestors, became arrogant and stiff-necked, and they did not obey your commands. They refused to listen and failed to remember the miracles you performed among them. They became stiff-necked and

*in their rebellion appointed a leader in order
to return to their slavery. But you are a
forgiving God, gracious and compassionate,
slow to anger and abounding in love.
Therefore, you did not desert them, even
when they cast for themselves an image of a
calf and said, 'This is your god, who brought
you up out of Egypt,' or when they committed
awful blasphemies."*

Fasting with Humility

After a great time of feasting, Israel found herself fasting with humility! This great contrast from joy to sorrow, however, was not a trip into *self-pity*. It was a trip into *the presence of God* to honestly see who God was and who they were ... to deal with the past in the present, and to keep from repeating those errors in the future!

It was healing oriented, not destructive self-pity! It was a sincere attempt to change and look to God for help, not just wallow in self-pity and complain!

The humility of the Israelites had to be both corporate *and* individual! When they agreed together to fast ... they each personally wore the apparel of genuine sorrow during their fast! This was not just another ritual ... it was serious business and the choice of each individual.

As it turned out, the entire camp joined together to analyze the errors of the past! The key here was to *examine* the past and acknowledge their sins ... but not to the point of self-pity. It was to learn! When the past steals our joy and envelopes us with self-pity or self-hatred, that is not the same thing as *humility!*

No one can make you humble ... you might be invited to be, but you must accept the invitation personally. This genuine humility revealed itself by the way the Israelites responded to the Word of God to separate themselves from all foreigners. This was not an arrogant "we are better than you" type of separation, but because God's Word had told them to be *different from the world!* This brings out a special point of real humility ... *obedience*, regular constant obedience!

Nehemiah 9:19-21

"Because of your great compassion you did not abandon them in the wilderness. By day the pillar of cloud did not fail to guide them on their path, nor the pillar of fire by night to shine on the way they were to take. You gave

your good Spirit to instruct them. You did not
withhold your manna from their mouths, and
you gave them water for their thirst. For forty
years you sustained them in the wilderness;
they lacked nothing, their clothes did not
wear out nor did their feet become swollen."

Recognition of Who God Is

It is interesting to note that they had spent three hours standing in place confessing their sins and those of their fathers! Notice they didn't start by confessing someone else's sins first! They started with their own sins!

It is easy (and arrogant) to ask God to reveal someone else's sin to you and to secondly ask God for your side of the sin! Real humility starts with *my* faults before leaning on *others'* faults! The next three hours, they listened to the Word of God ... a total of six hours in confession and instruction in the Word of God, along with healthy expressions of worship ... the second ingredient to proper humility ... *recognition of who God really is!*

The leaders are with the people in this. First, they confess their own sins. Then, they confess the sins of the past. Next, the character of God is affirmed by *worship!* Finally, the characteristics of God are alluded to in a long list.

The people cry, *"You are everlasting to everlasting"* ... God is timeless and forever! They acknowledge that they are temporal, creatures of the here and now, and can't even guess the future ... but *"You Lord are forever ... past, present, and future!"* This brought about a healthy respect for God. Reverence for the Lord is critical to genuine humility!

Acknowledging God

Who is it that really has provided everything we need? *God!* How arrogant man is about his accomplishments, rarely offering a word of acknowledgement about God's role in providing our needs. Even simple acknowledgements like praying before meals are going the way of the dodo bird, disappearing from families and homes around the world!

Notice the constant repetition of *"you"* for God:
- "You found"
- "You made"
- "You kept"
- "You saw"
- "You heard"
- "You sent"

- "You knew"
- "You divided"
- "You led"
- "You came down"
- "You spoke"
- "You gave"
- "You made known"

God has done so much ... yet we really acknowledge Him so little! The humble man doesn't forget history, especially what God has done in the past! God's past record of faithfulness *will* sustain the humble man!

Nehemiah 9:22-28

"You gave them kingdoms and nations,
allotting to them even the remotest frontiers.
They took over the country of Sihon king of
Heshbon and the country of Og king of
Bashan. You made their children as numerous
as the stars in the sky, and you brought them
into the land that you told their parents to
enter and possess. Their children went in and
took possession of the land. You subdued
before them the Canaanites, who lived in the
land; you gave the Canaanites into their

hands, along with their kings and the peoples of the land, to deal with them as they pleased. They captured fortified cities and fertile land; they took possession of houses filled with all kinds of good things, wells already dug, vineyards, olive groves and fruit trees in abundance. They ate to the full and were well-nourished; they reveled in your great goodness.

"But they were disobedient and rebelled against you; they turned their backs on your law. They killed your prophets, who had warned them in order to turn them back to you; they committed awful blasphemies. So you delivered them into the hands of their enemies, who oppressed them. But when they were oppressed they cried out to you. From heaven you heard them, and in your great compassion you gave them deliverers, who rescued them from the hand of their enemies.

"But as soon as they were at rest, they again did what was evil in your sight. Then you abandoned them to the hand of their enemies so that they ruled over them. And when they cried out to you again, you heard from

heaven, and in your compassion you delivered
them time after time."

Learning from the Past

Notice the change in tone and identities here: "*But they*, our forefathers ..." This should be the reason we look back at our sins or mistakes of the past ... not to *relive* the *guilt* of the past, but to *relieve* the guilt and *relearn* for the present and the future!

They recount the cyclical pattern of their fathers; thus, they are not just pointing their fingers at a particular group of failures, but to a cycle of failing! They are careful to include God's faithfulness all during these failures, too!

What's the lesson? ... *God is so great and His love so perfect that He is slow to anger and great in love* (v. 17).

What was the real problem with the past? *It was the arrogant striving to live without acknowledging God and His wonderful love!*

To ignore God's love and forgiveness is to live in *pride!* Pride is a form of self-reliance ... an "I don't need anybody else" mentality! This is a real cultural problem for the western world! We *pride* ourselves on how independent we are. This isn't always a healthy pride ... this can be arrogance! The truth is we *need God and one another!* God saw that when Adam was alone, *it was not good!*

What, then, was the lesson from the past? ... *Pride* had kept their fathers trapped in a lifestyle of sin that could only be shaken by repeated captivities under other godless nations ... in other words, to *humble* Israel, captivity would allow them to see their need of God! Arrogance is a type of captivity ... a bondage that is worse than an isolated prison cell ... it isolates *self!*

Nehemiah 9:29-31

"You warned them in order to turn them back to your law, but they became arrogant and disobeyed your commands. They sinned against your ordinances, of which you said, 'The person who obeys them will live by them.' Stubbornly they turned their backs on you, became stiff-necked and refused to listen. For many years you were patient with them. By your Spirit you warned them through your prophets. Yet they paid no attention, so you gave them into the hands of the neighboring peoples. But in your great mercy you did not put an end to them or

abandon them, for you are a gracious and merciful God."

The Warnings of God

Verse 29 contains a key statement — God had warned them, but in their arrogance, they had ignored the warnings. *God would warn Israel to stick with Scripture as their guide!* And arrogance was demonstrated when they didn't think they had to obey!

An important key to real humility is obedience! Biblical humility is not so much what *we want, but what God wants!* Learning to understand the Word and following it is the heart of humility!

Nehemiah 9:32-35

"Now therefore, our God, the great God, mighty and awesome, who keeps his covenant of love, do not let all this hardship seem trifling in your eyes—the hardship that has come on us, on our kings and leaders, on our priests and prophets, on our ancestors and all your people, from the days of the kings of Assyria until today. In all that has

happened to us, you have remained righteous; you have acted faithfully, while we acted wickedly. Our kings, our leaders, our priests and our ancestors did not follow your law; they did not pay attention to your commands or the statutes you warned them to keep. Even while they were in their kingdom, enjoying your great goodness to them in the spacious and fertile land you gave them, they did not serve you or turn from their evil ways."

Breaking the Cycle

Something is coming into focus here: *"Now therefore ..."* introduces a conclusion to all the comments that preceded this statement:

- God is an awesome ... great ... mighty ... God, *who keeps His promises!*
- God is a sure bet!
- Life is a gamble without God ... and the odds are zero if you bet against Him!

There had been a pattern for Israel in the past, one of cycles of disobedience and an unwillingness to learn from this constant cycle! Nothing can be sadder than someone who continues to make the same errors again and again! You can see them go from church to church to church ... always it's the church's fault, and perhaps at times it is, but a pattern emerges that produces an arrogance and bitterness that eats the joy right out of the heart of that saint!

However, God is faithful ... even to the misguided saint ... and when they truly become humble, God is able to let them see and understand ... and break the cycle!

In fact, knowing that God is so faithful in itself is often enough to break the bitter heart, even the arrogant spirit ... God's promises are yea and amen, and they bring healing to a hard heart!

Nehemiah 9:36-38

"But see, we are slaves today, slaves in the land you gave our ancestors so they could eat its fruit and the other good things it produces. Because of our sins, its abundant harvest goes to the kings you have placed over us. They rule over our bodies and our cattle as they please. We are in great distress

"In view of all this, we are making a binding agreement, putting it in writing, and our leaders, our Levites and our priests are

affixing their seals to it."

Petitioning God

Now that they had learned from their past errors, they were humbled to see the reality of their present status! So, they broke out with petitions ... but not just for blessings, for more things; they broke out with prayer that God would forgive their failings, not just their fathers'. They wanted their own sins forgiven! With this they acknowledged their total dependence upon God for their ultimate security!

The humble man of God recognizes that when the final call comes, it is God that gives us our sense of security! Their petition ends with, *"We are in great distress"* (v. 37).

What do they do after petitioning God for help and recognizing their utter dependence upon Him for forgiveness and help? They don't sit around and wait to see what God is going to do! The humble heart says, "Ok, what do I need to do now?" They respond while waiting for God to help them out of their distress by making a pledge to God ... not a foolish one, but a pledge carefully thought out and based on the lessons of the past!

This pledge would be their promise to walk with

God. The leaders took the role of being the example in this, but this pledge was an individual choice. All were invited to sign, but it was an individual choice!

This is still true with God. Your pastor can't get you into heaven, and you can't use him as an excuse for why you won't make it, either!

Why not walk with the best ... it doesn't get any better than God! Sign your name in the Book of Life with the rest of those who have learned from their past sins. Turn to the one who forgives all sin and renews your heart and mind! *Come to Christ*; join the covenant of God's people! *You can be healed of guilt, sin, and a sense of no purpose. God is waiting* for your pledge!

Real humility is a great healer – for it brings out the honest good and bad of our human nature and recognizes God's truly Holy nature! It also is honest about history – with the result of inspiring us in our hearts to live righteous lives in the present and future, while we learn from the past! God loves the truly humble heart; it is the true strength of a spiritually dynamic walk with God.

How humble are you?

FAITHFULNESS

Nehemiah 10:1-31

*Those who sealed it were ... the priests ... the
Levites ... the leaders of the people ... [and]
"The rest of the people—priests, Levites,
gatekeepers, musicians, temple servants and
all who separated themselves from the
neighboring peoples for the sake of the Law of
God, together with their wives and all their
sons and daughters who are able to
understand—all these now join their fellow
Israelites the nobles, and bind themselves with
a curse and an oath to follow the Law of God
given through Moses the servant of God and
to obey carefully all the commands,
regulations and decrees of the Lord our Lord.*

*"We promise not to give our daughters in
marriage to the peoples around us or take*

their daughters for our sons.

"When the neighboring peoples bring merchandise or grain to sell on the Sabbath, we will not buy from them on the Sabbath or on any holy day. Every seventh year we will forgo working the land and will cancel all debts."

The quality of "faithfulness" is the main structural support that holds up every institution. God has created and is an integral part of a healthy civilization! Faithfulness in our political system is a must for it to be healthy and beneficial ... when unfaithfulness manifests itself in any system, all kinds of ills will show up!

Marriage cannot exist without faithfulness as part of its main structure ... it is a pledge and commitment we make to the one we love.

Even the business sector has discovered the usefulness of having employees being faithful to their particular job area ... one of the things that has made the Japanese business system work so well.

No pain is greater than the loss of faithfulness ... whether in politics or in institutions, especially marriage and friendships! Unfortunately, the world's values don't always put a high priority on faithfulness.

Even when they say they do, they often practice "loopholes."

Faithfulness Is Critical

Faithfulness is one of the most critical factors in being a Christian ... without this quality, there is little hope for spiritual growth or fulfillment! Many Christians miss the joy of being a growing saint and being able to see fruit from their ministry because of the lack of faithfulness in their walk with God and with each other!

We cannot mature spiritually without learning the absolute necessity of faithfulness in all relationships ... especially in the institutions God has created, including our relationship with Him! *Faithfulness* and *fruitfulness* go hand in hand. Without one, the other rarely exists!

It was critical at this juncture that the leaders of the people took the initiative to seal with their own seals a proclamation to declare their willingness to be absolutely faithful to God's Word! This was true of the secular leaders and the spiritual leaders ... which in this case were often the same, like Nehemiah.

A Lack of Heroes

These leadership positions can have a tremendous impact on the people they govern! One of the problems cited in a special article in *Time* magazine in July 1990 concerned the twenty-year-old age group. They had grown up without heroes, and that had robbed their passion. They were less focused on important issues than those in previous generations.

Political heroes of the 1960s – John F. Kennedy, Bobby Kennedy, Martin Luther King Jr., etc. became the focal points that provided the passion for the younger generation in the sixties and early seventies. The point is not whether these were good role models or the reactions were all healthy ... but that heroes existed, to which a young person could become committed, producing a faithful following!

God help us ... we need to have spiritual role models to inspire the younger generation ... to give passion to important issues of our day!

Key Qualities of Leaders

One of the key qualities of church leaders is that they must be faithful to inspire the rest of God's people! The role models in Nehemiah's day set an important standard within the community of God's people

... and fruitfulness and revival weren't far away!

Because of the role models' expression of sealing their commitment of faithfulness, all Israel, from the youngest person who could understand, joined in binding themselves to be faithful to God's Word ... accepting the curses and the blessings that could come with either disobedience or obedience! Their passion was obvious! Their joy was obvious ... and their determination that they could be faithful. We see it expressed by the fact that they were even willing to accept the curses of disobedience should they fail!

Everyone is ready to accept the fruit that comes with faithfulness ... but I wonder how many today willingly accept the curses that come with disobedience? The children of Israel were not anticipating failure ... their confidence level was high! The curses didn't seem an obstacle to them since their hearts were filled with the passion of faithfulness!

When we marry someone, we do the same thing ... we are not thinking about the consequences of unfaithfulness, yet we passionately state our willingness to forsake all others and cleave only unto our spouse. The ceremony of marriage is a joyful one ... and a bit of a gamble. We are gambling on the equal desire of our partner to remain faithful to that pledge of faithfulness!

Nehemiah 10:32-36

"We assume the responsibility for carrying out the commands to give a third of a shekel each year for the service of the house of our God: for the bread set out on the table; for the regular grain offerings and burnt offerings; for the offerings on the Sabbaths, at the New Moon feasts and at the appointed festivals; for the holy offerings; for sin offerings to make atonement for Israel; and for all the duties of the house of our God.

"We—the priests, the Levites and the people— have cast lots to determine when each of our families is to bring to the house of our God at set times each year a contribution of wood to burn on the altar of the Lord our God, as it is written in the Law.

"We also assume responsibility for bringing to the house of the Lord each year the first fruits of our crops and of every fruit tree.

"As it is also written in the Law, we will bring the firstborn of our sons and of our cattle, of

our herds and of our flocks to the house of our
God, to the priests ministering there."

A Commitment to Faithfulness

The commitment to faithfulness is stated in the general sense ... *"We will obey all the decrees of the Lord ..."* Overall, there is a broad sense of excitement among the people about being faithful. The desire to be faithful should spark a general excitement ... but there must be specific attitudes and specific directions in place to make faithfulness work in your life. You must move from the general to the specific! This is a normal process. This stage of *aspiring to faithfulness* was only a beginning ... the next step was to apply this desire to some real areas of their lives!

Too many Christians are more than happy to express their desire to be faithful to God but then never go the next step and develop a new mentality ... to begin changing so that faithfulness can find a *full expression* in their daily lives and not just a verbal one!

Notice the people move to this second stage very quickly ... the passion to be faithful to God now finds some specific directions, not just a general statement! These areas of repentance were areas of their failures! They repent of their failure to stay pure as a people before God by unbiblical marriages. They vow to honor the Sabbath day as a holy day and not just as another opportunity to make more profits! And they swear obedience to the "rest" God decreed for the land every seven years. This also included the pardoning every seven years of all their brethren's debts ... something Nehemiah had chided them for earlier because they were charging heavy interest to their poorer brethren and taking their children when the loans were not paid in full! This was a whole change of attitude for the people ... each of the items listed were the actual areas where they needed to repent. They didn't complain about other people's unfaithfulness ... but focused on their own need to repent for their own unfaithfulness!

An Attitude of Repentance

The attitude of repentance of one's *own unfaithfulness* is the next stage of growth. Too many Christians begin this stage by pointing out other people's lack of faithfulness ... this will only block their own growth!

Notice the attitude of the people's emerging faithfulness ... *"We assume the responsibility ..."* Personal responsibility is a must in the expression of faithfulness. To look at others and complain about them will only put you on a spiritual detour away from your own faithfulness. Pointing at other Christians' faults reveals a truth about us: We have failed to develop the right attitude over faithfulness.

When we stand before God, we will have to answer for why or why we were not faithful to Him ... and using other people's good or bad examples won't wash with God! Faithfulness is a personal responsibility ... nobody else can be used as our excuse for unfaithfulness no matter what they have done! Healthy faithfulness says, "*I assume responsibility for carrying out God's Word ...*"

A repentant attitude will create within us a sense of personal responsibility! The trouble with some Christians is that they focus too much on the faults of others and then judge their own faithfulness against those whom they judge to be failures. They try to make themselves feel less guilty (or see no need to become more faithful themselves, which is arrogance). The right attitude of faithfulness is the repentance of personal failures and the acceptance of personal responsibility for being faithful, no matter who or what is around them as examples!

Jesus' response someday will be, "Well done, thou

good and faithful servant ... enter ..." Notice that Jesus doesn't compare you with anyone else. He simply takes notice of *your faithfulness!*

Nehemiah 10:37-39

"Moreover, we will bring to the storerooms of the house of our God, to the priests, the first of our ground meal, of our grain offerings, of the fruit of all our trees and of our new wine and olive oil. And we will bring a tithe of our crops to the Levites, for it is the Levites who collect the tithes in all the towns where we work. A priest descended from Aaron is to accompany the Levites when they receive the tithes, and the Levites are to bring a tenth of the tithes up to the house of our God, to the storerooms of the treasury. The people of Israel, including the Levites, are to bring their contributions of grain, new wine and olive oil to the storerooms, where the articles for the sanctuary and for the ministering priests, the gatekeepers and the musicians are also kept.

"We will not neglect the house of our God."

Also Needed: Action!

The process of faithfulness is not complete if we stop at the desire to be faithful or even the attitude of faithfulness ... it must reach the final stage of *action!* Faithfulness takes great resolve ... it is not just a verbal expression ... it is a way of life ... a constant commitment that is made every day ... day in and day out!

The commitments the Jews were making were regular and routine ... year after year after year! It is easy to make a commitment to God to be faithful in an altar call when your emotions are fully engaged, but the real test of commitment comes in the weeks that follow as the daily grind and routine of life wears at us. It takes resolve to remain faithful when the emotional factors are either not present or they run contrary to our commitment of faithfulness!

Their resolve was a full one ... to call upon each other to be faithful and obedient ... each one doing their part. Their faithfulness included such items as attendance, giving, proper and rightful respect for God's authorities, and the reestablishment of order that honors God through their mouths and through their wallets!

As time passed, they would enjoy the fruit of their

faithfulness in greater and greater measure. The fruit of their actions would be God's presence and His blessings upon them as a nation. They would also rediscover the joy that comes from being part of God's unique people ... their resolve was real ... and it had a real expression to it!

Commitment to the Temple

One area of expression was their faithfulness to God and His temple. They once again laid a proper order for the temple of God and committed their resources (already stretched to the limit as mentioned in the earlier passages). Although later the temple tax would be set at half a shekel, for now it was put at a third (v. 32), probably to help them in their extreme poverty!

The point here is that they returned to being faithful by faithful expression of their resources! One sign of the faithful saint is how they are faithful to serve God with their resources and their gifts! Faithfulness cannot minister to others if there are no real expressions to it. It's like our own modern proverb: *"Action speaks louder than words!"*

Moving Towards Maturity

Faithfulness in aspiration, in attitude, and finally in action reflects the saint of God who is moving toward or in maturity! This can often explain why some Christians sit still and do not grow while other Christians seem to thrive and grow! Faithfulness is often the key that makes the difference!

The key to spiritual power and maturity is found in a single word: *faithfulness!* The problem of spiritual dryness is never the result of God's failure to be faithful, or the faults and errors of other Christians ... they are the responsibility of our commitment to being faithful before God! It is faithfulness that separates the successful saints from the unsuccessful ones ... not the results of ministry. The Bible even recognizes the sad rarity of this quality in Proverbs 20:6 in The Message Bible:

Lots of people claim to be loyal and loving, but where on earth can you find one?

Faithfulness needs to be the rule. How about you ... are you the rule or the exception?

A Healthy Body

Nehemiah 11:1-2

Now the leaders of the people settled in Jerusalem. The rest of the people cast lots to bring one out of every ten of them to live in Jerusalem, the holy city, while the remaining nine were to stay in their own towns. The people commended all who volunteered to live in Jerusalem.

David said it best in Psalms 139:14.

I praise you because I am fearfully and wonderfully made; your works are wonderful, I know that full well.

The human body is the most amazing machine on the planet. It has literally multiple billions of cells ...

and a large quantity of them are doing different things at different times and at the same time ... each dependent on the other, unique in function, equal in existence!

We only seem to take notice of this marvelous order of life when it goes chaotic ... such as when cancer strikes; cells that multiply out of control. It is ironic that such a disease like cancer can kill us ... for it is our own cells doing what they are supposed to do, but not in their orderly fashion. They just take off and grow and grow until they take over the nourishment demands of the body and crowd out or eat away other important parts – the body then itself dies *and ironically the cancer dies with it!* It quite literally kills itself along with all the other healthy tissue that struggles to keep order within the body!

We could not exist very well without order ... God Himself is a God of order ... we only have to examine nature and the skies at night to understand how true this is.

Life Without Order

Imagine life without order! What if the law of gravity couldn't be counted on ... *one day you are up ... then next day you are down* – literally! Imagine time without an order to it ... you couldn't plan out any-thing for even a day, much less make a weekly sched-ule ... *you wouldn't know when church started or stopped!*

What if there was no order in our banking institu-tions? Billions of dollars might disappear and cause the collapse of thousands of savings and loans institu-tions!

No matter what you are talking about, order is necessary for all things to exist in a healthy state, or to be useful. This includes the church! God made our natural bodies to have order within them, and He has also established His supernatural Body, the church, to have order within it! This extends not only to the administrative structure of the church; but also, the spiritual life of the church ... worship unstructured or without order can bring chaos.

God is not against planning or structure; indeed, His Word is full of instances where He blessed plans and structure as long as there was also proper room and recognition of His authority and freedom to move within that structure or order!

A Model of Order

Nehemiah was directing a call for a tenth of the

people across the nation to move into Jerusalem. It was time for the world to sit up and take notice of God's City!

While this was a common practice for the nations of the day to grow new cities with a sampling of people from across the nation, creating a "mini" nation within the city, Jerusalem was to be a model not of man, but of God and His glory. This was the point of having the holy temple within the holy city! Rather than have a man – or a civic building – at the center of Jerusalem, God would reside in the center of the city!

Jerusalem would once again be called the *"Holy City"* ... it was to be a unique model of God's kingdom alive within an entire city. This model city would be comprised of the rulers and also a tithe of the people from the nation! Lots were cast in each community of Israel, and one out of every ten citizens would be asked to relocate into this model city-society called Jerusalem! For those who had the lot fall to them, it very literally could mean moving to a smaller home and leaving behind the wealth they were earning on a productive farm! For many of those whose lot fell on them, this move proved to be a downward financial turn. Nevertheless, they were obedient to lose something for being a privileged citizen of the "Holy

City!" Some things were considered by these people as greater than the things of this world. Sounds like a great sermon here alone!

One day this will again be true ... when the holy city, the New Jerusalem, comes down from heaven and we will be her citizens, those who know Christ as Lord!

The New Jerusalem will be the perfect model that it failed to be in the Old Testament!

Burning for the Lord

Some commentators believe that Nehemiah was trying to establish this "mini-nation" with a tenth of the whole of Israel within Jerusalem ... to be God's tithe people, a special people to model a special holy city! There were some men who didn't need a "lucky chance" lot to fall to them ... their hearts were so aflame with jealousy for the Lord their God that they volunteered to move and leave behind their fortunes to live within God's city! There are always some people who don't have to be drafted for ministry. They step forward and volunteer to meet the need! The rest of Israel's response to these eager saints was not *jealousy*; it was *rejoicing* ... the rest of Israel blessed these volunteers!

The volunteers' example set the community to rejoicing and fired up the others that God was on the move within their holy community – as well as took some of the pressure off the lottery system! Not as many had to be chosen, because of those who had volunteered.

This is still true today within God's temple (the church). You will find men and women of this caliber who inspire others to serve the Lord and excite the church. This should always be the case with the church's leaders!

It still seems statistically true that about 10% of God's people do 90% of the work ... but beyond the tithe of people, we could still use more volunteers!

Fighting Men

The first group of people recorded besides the provincial leaders and various servants of Solomon were a company called the "descendants of Perez," described as *"468 able men."* The meaning of this phrase in Hebrew is *"strong men,"* or ... *"outstanding men"* ... probably in the sense of military men or fighters!

Why did a holy city need warriors? Because there will always be enemies ready to destroy God's work and His people! I pray that God will give us warriors in the church today, those who will fight against the enemy that tries to destroy the church of God! "To contend for the faith" was the cry in the heart of Jude. He wrote in Jude 3:

I ... urge you to contend for the faith that was once for all entrusted to the saints.

Being a Christian citizen of the New Jerusalem includes the need for warriors of the faith ... those who will contend for the faith! God give us *a godly militia* ... these are the ones gifted for vanquishing the enemy before the enemy has a chance to harm anyone within the holy city!

In other places in the Bible, we are called to endure hardship as a good soldier of Jesus Christ. 2 Timothy 2:3 encourages us to "*Endure hardship with us like a good soldier of Christ Jesus.*"

Nehemiah 11:3-14

These are the provincial leaders who settled in Jerusalem (now some Israelites, priests, Levites, temple servants and descendants of Solomon's servants lived in the towns of Judah, each on their own property in the various towns, while other people from both Judah and Benjamin lived in Jerusalem):

From the descendants of Judah:

Athaiah son of Uzziah, the son of Zechariah, the son of Amariah, the son of Shephatiah, the son of Mahalalel, a descendant of Perez; and Maaseiah son of Baruch, the son of Kol-Hozeh, the son of Hazaiah, the son of Adaiah, the son of Joiarib, the son of Zechariah, a descendant of Shelah. The descendants of Perez who lived in Jerusalem totaled 468 men of standing.

From the descendants of Benjamin:

Sallu son of Meshullam, the son of Joed, the son of Pedaiah, the son of Kolaiah, the son of Maaseiah, the son of Ithiel, the son of Jeshaiah, and his followers, Gabbai and Sallai—928 men. Joel son of Zikri was their chief officer, and Judah son of Hassenuah was over the New Quarter of the city.

From the priests:

Jedaiah; the son of Joiarib; Jakin; Seraiah son of Hilkiah, the son of Meshullam, the son of

Zadok, the son of Meraioth, the son of Ahitub,
the official in charge of the house of God, and
their associates, who carried on work for the
temple—822 men; Adaiah son of Jeroham, the
son of Pelaliah, the son of Amzi, the son of
Zechariah, the son of Pashhur, the son of
Malkijah, and his associates, who were heads
of families—242 men; Amashsai son of Azarel,
the son of Ahzai, the son of Meshillemoth, the
son of Immer, and his associates, who were
men of standing—128. Their chief officer was
Zabdiel son of Haggedolim.

Officers and Elders

In verse 9, a man called Joel was listed as the "chief officer" over one area, and another by the name of Judah was listed as chief officer over the second district ... a new suburb of the holy city. The term used here, "chief officer," meant in Hebrew an "overseer" (the role of an elder within the New Testament church).

God called out some men to be elders in the holy temple to supervise and oversee the spiritual concerns of the people ... citizens to soldiers! It is interesting to note that there were several of these men, the two I just mentioned above, and in verse 11, Seraiah (also called Azuria) as the chief supervisor (or overseer) of the temple itself!

Note that Seraiah had several associate pastors serving with him because of the size of the community!

Last, the area of old Jerusalem also needed an "overseer" or elder, and Zabdiel is listed at the end of verse 14. Zabdiel probably oversaw the area within the city itself as its elder. This sounds similar to a modern church, with at least 3 elders over various territories and a chief or senior pastor over the temple itself, comprising a *board of elders!*

The church needs godly elders, men who can lay aside their egos and ideas and find the mind of Christ ... mindful always that the church is God's temple, and they are instructed to oversee it for Him!

Nehemiah 11:15-18

From the Levites:

Shemaiah son of Hasshub, the son of Azrikam, the son of Hashabiah, the son of Bunni; Shabbethai and Jozabad,two of the heads of the Levites, who had charge of the outside work of the house of God; Mattaniah son of

Mika, the son of Zabdi, the son of Asaph, the director who led in thanksgiving and prayer; Bakbukiah, second among his associates; and Abda son of Shammua, the son of Galal, the son of Jeduthun. The Levites in the holy city totaled 284.

A New Group of Workers: Deacons

Nehemiah was setting up the church in a very orderly way! This was no half-baked organization thrown together in a moment of whimsey. A new group is introduced in this section, men who had charge of the *"outside work of the house of God."* Their responsibilities were to take care to see that all the facilities were kept up and all needed supplies were on site.

This was much less glamorous than the jobs of the overseers ... but it was critical to the worship experience! The idea in the Hebrew is similar to the New Testament role of *deacons!* They were to take care of the material assistance and duties needed for the temple of God to operate properly! They would relieve the pressures from the overseers, chief officers and ministers so they could concentrate on the demands of the people's spiritual needs.

While not glamorous work ... done properly it caused the resulting *praise and thanksgiving* we read about in verse 17. The congregation could not have given thanks if adequate supplies had not been present!

The role of these early deacons allowed the entire temple to run smoothly, so that the focus in the temple could be off things and on God! Their function and call were critical to the needs of the holy temple ... and this is still true with *deacons!* Nehemiah was creating a model of the New Testament temple, the church, but in his own day!

These "deacons" managed the affairs of the church that were on the practical side, less glamorous than the public role of the elders ... but equal in importance for the whole temple to function properly!

Nehemiah 11:19-20

The gatekeepers:

Akkub, Talmon and their associates, who kept watch at the gates—172 men.

The rest of the Israelites, with the priests and Levites, were in all the towns of Judah, each on their ancestral property.

A Call for Gatekeepers

There were some other men who served as "gate-keepers" ... possibly manning the gates of the temple, not the city gates. These were deacons who served in roles something like our *ushers* today! They lived on the hill of Ophel near the temple area ... their duties included guarding the treasures and sacred items within the temple, a function similar to deacons, but much like *ushers, too* (or trustees). Notice there was even a *chief usher!* Ziha and Gishpa were the *head ushers!*

A very familiar order was developing around the temple and the holy city ... one that would bring *order* to the body; it was needed if they hoped to prove they were the chosen people of God!

Nehemiah 11:21-23

The temple servants lived on the hill of Ophel, and Ziha and Gishpa were in charge of them.

The chief officer of the Levites in Jerusalem was Uzzi son of Bani, the son of Hashabiah,

the son of Mattaniah, the son of Mika. Uzzi
was one of Asaph's descendants, who were
the musicians responsible for the service of the
house of God. The musicians were under the
king's orders, which regulated their daily
activity.

A Special Provision for the Choir

They also had an entire choir. The king provided daily provisions for the members so that they might spend their entire time in the ministry of music! (Boy, wouldn't this be nice today!) "Uzzi a descendant of Asaph," the famous song writer of David's time, became the new choir director! Why would a secular king give financial support for a religious choir? It was common in that day for a conquered race (and Jerusalem was under the authority of King Artaxerxes) to sing a blessing upon the king and his future children so the land would be prosperous and at peace. Uzzi was happy to do this, and it benefited the choir as well.

The temple of God was filled with musicians praising and worshiping the God of Heaven ... this enhanced the worship experience! Music is a major part of a worship experience ... it prepares our hearts and minds for the Word of God that will be spoken later!

What made it nice here is that this choir could and did practice daily for the temple worship service! *Preparation of songs is critical to the experience of worship!* What a plan ... *elders, deacons, ushers, spiritual warriors, and now musicians!* Sounds pretty modern, doesn't it!? Music plays a critical role with our worship experience ... and it should have great planning behind it. Plus, in the case of choir or specials, *practice is vital!* There is nothing sacred about just "winging it."

Nehemiah 11:24

Pethahiah son of Meshezabel, one of the descendants of Zerah son of Judah, was the king's agent in all affairs relating to the people.

A Unique Post

One man held a unique post. He was to be the mediator between God's people and King Artaxerxes.

The New Testament comparison is obvious ... It is Jesus Christ alone who is the mediator between the

King of Kings and the people ... it is He that alone mediates the church's experience and needs to our Heavenly King!

The mediator's role is vital to New Jerusalem and its citizens! In the days of Nehemiah, conquering kings rebuilt the temples of their subjected people in the hopes that the gods of the subjected people would bless them ... our conquering King Jesus has provided everything we need for His holy temple, the church, and He is still our mediator between God and man!

Nehemiah 11:25-30

As for the villages with their fields, some of the people of Judah lived in Kiriath Arba and its surrounding settlements, in Dibon and its settlements, in Jekabzeel and its villages, in Jeshua, in Moladah, in Beth Pelet, in Hazar Shual, in Beersheba and its settlements, in Ziklag, in Mekonah and its settlements, in En Rimmon, in Zorah, in Jarmuth, Zanoah, Adullam and their villages, in Lachish and its fields, and in Azekah and its settlements. So they were living all the way from Beersheba to the Valley of Hinnom.

Reclaiming Our Lost Inheritance

This list also tells of God's people scattered abroad in the land, not living in the New Jerusalem full time! Their purpose was to eventually fill the land with their numbers, so that without war, they might one day reclaim the land that once belonged to them!

They had spread out beyond the old borders with settlements into enemy territory, unafraid to settle, confident that their brethren would come to their aid when and if it became necessary to fight to keep their land!

They once again believed God's promises for the land to be theirs! Ironically, this is still pretty much the policy of Israel even today, to build settlements within occupied territory. Even though the enemy complains, by the time the legal system works through the paperwork, they hope to have a majority of their people living there and to claim possession by right of numbers!

The church could learn from this ... *Our life should not just be in* occupying the *temple* (the church) – *We need to spread out around the areas we live in and win those people to Christ, thus increasing the population of saints in those particular areas!*

We are to be salt penetrating society to bring

healing to it ... salt also prevents the rotting of food; our presence should have a healthy constraint on the expression of evil as more and more saints live within a community!

This is much like Jesus' call for us to spread the gospel to "Jerusalem, Judea, Samaria, and to the uttermost parts of the world!" *Spread out,* Saints, and attack the area you live in, or settle in and win so many that an attack will be unnecessary. The saints will just take over by sheer numbers!

We cannot be content to live in the holy temple we call the church. We must be the church in the world ... they need to see the people of God and what we are ... how we are different!

Nehemiah 11:31-36

The descendants of the Benjamites from Geba lived in Mikmash, Aija, Bethel and its settlements, in Anathoth, Noband Ananiah, in Hazor, Ramah and Gittaim, in Hadid, Zeboim and Neballat, in Lod and Ono, and in Ge Harashim.

Some of the divisions of the Levites of Judah settled in Benjamin.

The Final List

This final list names some from one tribe living in the territories of other tribes ... there were some who were mixed up; Israel was becoming more of a melting pot, people with unique identities living around those who were different from them, even though some of these were their own brethren!

Let's face it, the holy temple of the church today deals with the same issue. We are all God's people. Some of us come from the city, some have lived in one spot all their lives, some are highly educated (others not as much), some from the South, some are outright Yankees ... but no matter, *we are the church!* It should be a blessing to exist within this melting pot ... we can all benefit from each other ... even though we don't all have the same backgrounds!

A healthy church is not one without conflicts ... it is one, however, where conflicts are healed by loving, committed saints who are trying to meld together into one Body of Christ!

Nehemiah's leaders weren't flawless ... neither were the people ... but God was creating out of them a unique group of people, a people called by *His Name.*

All this order was to help smooth the process for God's Spirit to work within a body that was coordinated and functioning in harmony! This is the point for the church. We are His body ... and if healthy, the Head will be able to use us to bring honor and glory to His name ... even though we serve in different places. Being connected to the body and not fighting the other parts will allow a healthy body to function under the impulses of the Head.

Growing a Healthy Church

All this requires a great deal of planning and practicing. *Healthy life doesn't just grow in erratic ways, it grows in an orderly fashion!* Order doesn't destroy the work of the Spirit in a worship service. It enhances the Spirit's ability to speak in an orderly way for the best results ... God is a God of order, not chaos!

All healthy living organisms have order in them – cancer is the result of healthy cells becoming disorderly and growing chaotically, thus producing disease, and if unchecked – death! A healthy church (called by the New Testament a living body) is only healthy when it is operating in an orderly fashion. Worship too should be carefully planned and thought out! This enhances our worship experience; it does not inhibit or restrict it! Without a well-structured body, the head cannot issue useful signals that demonstrate healthy life or movement. The point of structure is to give coordinated movement toward the head's goals! Our God of *order* finds it difficult to work through a *chaotic* and unstructured body!

Thankfulness

Nehemiah 12:27-30

At the dedication of the wall of Jerusalem, the Levites were sought out from where they lived and were brought to Jerusalem to celebrate joyfully the dedication with songs of thanksgiving and with the music of cymbals, harps and lyres. The musicians also were brought together from the region around Jerusalem—from the villages of the Netophathites, from Beth Gilgal, and from the area of Geba and Azmaveth, for the musicians had built villages for themselves around Jerusalem. When the priests and Levites had purified themselves ceremonially, they purified the people, the gates and the wall.

Perhaps the most powerful and most undervalued attitude of the human heart is thankfulness!

America (and much of the modern world) has much to be thankful for. We live luxurious lifestyles by the standards of the past, with comfortable homes, good cars, and a multitude of electronic devices. The irony about having so much is that those with the most blessings are often the very ones that consider them their right! They've worked for them, so why should they be thankful?

A Very Powerful Influence

The virtue of thankfulness influences all other virtues and attitudes of life ... thus it is the most powerful virtue of all!

Psalm 92:1 states: "It is good to praise the Lord, and make music to your name ..." and in Psalm 100:4, "Enter his gates with thanksgiving, and his courts with praise; give thanks to him and praise his name!"

Ephesians 5:20 tell us: "Always giving thanks to God the Father for everything ..." Colossians 2:7 says we are to be "... overflowing with thankfulness!"

In 1 Thessalonians 5:18, the Word says to: "Give thanks in all circumstances, for this is God's will for you in Christ Jesus." And let's not forget Hebrews 13:15: "Through Jesus, therefore, let us continually offer to God a sacrifice of praise ... the fruit of lips that confess His name."

One of the most powerful influences in a Christian's life is *thankfulness*. Without it, life is filled with bitterness and nothing satisfies the heart ... with it, a believer's life only gets better. Satisfaction and contentment permeate every circumstance. Thankfulness is the one virtue that deeply influences all other Christian virtues! *Thanklessness destroys the soul ... thankfulness delivers the soul!*

Nehemiah 12:31-37

I had the leaders of Judah go up on top of the wall. I also assigned two large choirs to give thanks. One was to proceed on top of the wall to the right, toward the Dung Gate. Hoshaiah and half the leaders of Judah followed them, along with Azariah, Ezra, Meshullam, Judah, Benjamin, Shemaiah, Jeremiah, as well as some priests with trumpets, and also Zechariah son of Jonathan, the son of Shemaiah, the son of Mattaniah, the son of Micaiah, the son of Zakkur, the son of Asaph, and his associates—Shemaiah, Azarel, Milalai, Gilalai, Maai, Nethanel, Judah and Hanani—

with musical instruments prescribed by David the man of God. Ezra the teacher of the Law led the procession. At the Fountain Gate they continued directly up the steps of the City of David on the ascent to the wall and passed above the site of David's palace to the Water Gate on the east.

Music Leads the Way

From the beginning of man's experience of worship, music has always led the way! Music is one of the most potent forms of communication and one of the most powerful influences on the human soul and mind ... it can quite literally shape and alter our moods and emotions and affect our will and behavior!

Even the devil understands the power of music. Satan uses music to influence the lives and minds of people in a negative way! We're not talking about the style of music people listen to, but the message they get through the music. Music reaches us through our emotions – for good or bad. When we are attracted to the music – whatever style it is – we become open to the content of the lyrics and the message the music portrays.

There is no such thing as unemotional music! We

will be affected one way or another. Music can be *uplifting or damning!* That is why it is so important to pay attention to the music we surround ourselves with.

In Jerusalem, the singers were living throughout the city, making Jerusalem a city literally surrounded by sound! The singers had built their houses and villages around Jerusalem (v. 29 says: "... for the singers had built villages for themselves around Jerusalem."). Can you imagine this scene? The holy city had surround-sound music! Imagine waking up in the holy city with the sounds of music from everywhere around you, the music of worship!

King David knew the power of music. David playing his harp under the inspiration of the Holy Spirit was the only thing that could calm an evil King Saul. David celebrated the return of the ark of God with the sound of trumpets and music! It was the singers who were usually first in line on the battlefield!!! They often led Israel into battle! (It must have worked. Otherwise, it would have limited people's desire to be in the choir!)

Nehemiah 12:38-39

The second choir proceeded in the opposite direction. I followed them on top of the wall,

*together with half the people—past the Tower
of the Ovens to the Broad Wall, over the Gate
of Ephraim, the Jeshanah Gate, the Fish Gate,
the Tower of Hananel and the Tower of the
Hundred, as far as the Sheep Gate. At the Gate
of the Guard they stopped.*

Preparing to Sing

Along with the music, there was a preparing pro-cess ... to make everything clean and pure! Why can't we get into worship during a song service sometimes? *Have we prepared* our hearts to do so before arriving ... by being clean and purified from anger, malice, hatred, bitterness, etc.!?

Sacred music is a waste of time without making sure everything else is sacred! You get out of a wor-ship experience exactly what you put into it ... or how prepared you are when you arrive! Fight on the way to church in the car and see how well you think the service goes or how well the preacher preached! Be angry with someone and let unforgiveness rule in your heart, and then try to experience the joy of wor-ship!!

Much of the atmosphere of a worship experience depends on what happens before we arrive ... and is reflected in how we arrive! Preparation of the heart is a whole lot more important than the suit and tie you put on – or the make-up that took an hour to apply before getting there ... *better to make-up* with God and be *tied* to your brethren first. Then you are *well-suited* for worship!

Nehemiah 12:40-43

The two choirs that gave thanks then took their places in the house of God; so, did I, together with half the officials, as well as the priests—Eliakim, Maaseiah, Miniamin, Micaiah, Elioenai, Zechariah and Hananiah with their trumpets—and also Maaseiah, Shemaiah, Eleazar, Uzzi, Jehohanan, Malkijah, Elam and Ezer. The choirs sang under the direction of Jezrahiah. And on that day they offered great sacrifices, rejoicing because God had given them great joy. The women and children also rejoiced. The sound of rejoicing in Jerusalem could be heard far away.

Finding Joy through Song

What was so fascinating about the choir breaking

into two groups and going in opposite directions on the walls until they met ... all the while singing? They would each be singing when they came to the section of the wall they had worked on! Joy would whelm up in their hearts as they walked over the very spot they had labored over ... their music would soar as their feet covered that very spot!

Their music — and the joy they received through their songs – was based on thankfulness for what God had done in the past, especially the recent past! If we fail to remember the good things of God when we are experiencing tough times, we will fail to be thankful! Memory of what God has already done for us must be stirred to enable us to be thankful even during a trial. We need to see the bigger picture when we are locked into a small tunnel and suffering!

A List of the Workers

We read a list of the individuals who helped plan this time of *thankfulness!* Why is this important? *It's when we participate in being thankful that we receive the most joy!*

There are two levels of experience in worship: the corporate dynamic and the individual dynamic. One must participate in being thankful to experience any joy in worship! You can't ride on other people's thankfulness or joy ... you need to join in with them! While walking the walls singing with *thanksgiving* was itself a wonderful experience, their destination was the *house of God* where they met and *joined in thanksgiving!* Thanksgiving must be pressed *into our memories ... and that occurs with our participation in expressing thanksgiving in the house of God!*

A Goal of Ministry

Each musician took their place of ministry when they joined at the *house of God!* Singing on the wall was wonderful ... the antiphonal choir music uplifting and moving ... but the goal was ministry! The most thankful tend to be the most involved in ministry, primarily because thankful people do not find sacrificing difficult ... they are grateful to be used by God! Unthankful hearts tend to think of their own needs first and find little that they can sacrifice!

As the musicians took their position in God's temple, they blessed the whole group. Everyone was filled with joy and thanksgiving! The individual was blessed by their contribution – *the individual dynamic of worship* – and the whole group joined in being thankful – *the corporate dynamic of worship.* They experienced *worship that demonstrated its joy in giving ... the very expression of thanks is that of joyful giving!*

Nehemiah 12:44-47

At that time men were appointed to be in charge of the storerooms for the contributions, first fruits and tithes. From the fields around the towns they were to bring into the storerooms the portions required by the Law for the priests and the Levites, for Judah was pleased with the ministering priests and Levites. They performed the service of their God and the service of purification, as did also the musicians and gatekeepers, according to the commands of David and his son Solomon. For long ago, in the days of David and Asaph, there had been directors for the musicians and for the songs of praise and thanksgiving to God. So in the days of Zerubbabel and of Nehemiah, all Israel contributed the daily portions for the musicians and the gatekeepers. They also set aside the portion for the other Levites, and the Levites set aside the portion for the descendants of Aaron.

Beyond Average

Joy in worship leads to joy in giving. Giving becomes an expression of joy. The worshippers in Jerusalem weren't satisfied with middle-of-the-road giving ... they went beyond the average! They had already done this in their thanksgiving of song as they walked the walls (sounds like old time Pentecostals!). This was no time for a mediocre attitude toward giving!

The expression of thanksgiving took on very practical aspects! Each person did their part and everyone was taken care of! There was enough for the priests, the Levites and the other appointed places of ministry. And the people in ministry also had their needs supplied!

This was all practical and down to earth! No flights of fancy here. The house of God had what was needed to stay in shape. The servants of full-time ministry were properly taken care of. When the need arose for those within Israel who found themselves in need, the proper necessities were supplied from the house of God.

The biggest part of *beyond average* is found in the attitude of the people. The giving didn't have to be coerced ... thankfulness had created an *atmosphere of generosity*, and the Levites were kept busy properly taking care of and storing the sacrifices of the people to God's house! No more worrying about money ... there was no lack ... all the time and efforts of the ministry team could be placed on ministry, not finding money to run the ministerial programs!

The idea in this final verse is that *thankfulness* had practical expression to it! Why not write a note of thanksgiving to someone you appreciate? Find some way to tell someone you are thankful for them. They may not be perfect (Who is?) but you can show that you appreciate them, anyway!

A Warning

The people were pleased with the ministry of their priests and Levites! In other words, they got something out of the priests' ministry. And the choir of the Levites blessed their souls!

There will be a complete reversal of this attitude in the next chapter ... which has Nehemiah back at the king's palace and gone from Jerusalem for several years. During this time, the people lose their thankfulness ... and they lose their appreciation of each other's ministries! Nehemiah must return and reinvigorate ministry by and to the people.

An Example from Today

Good ministry (and our attitude of thankfulness) has more to do with how much we put into it than how well the preacher preached! I have taught what I considered an average sermon and had people tell me how much it ministered to them!

It was a surprise to me, probably because I wasn't thankful for the job I did. I was aware of my short-comings, but they were grateful to hear God's Word. Their words of appreciation changed how I felt about my sermon – and my ability to do a good job when I let God take charge of the service! I'm also more aware of how important my preparation time is. People are blessed by the message when God is in it, but the better my preparation is, the more God can bless them!

You can almost feel the excitement in the city of God (the church) ... great celebration, great thank-fulness ... great joy in ministry. It is a joy to minister to one another when each minister is appreciated! A word of appreciation can bring more healing and create more commitment toward ministry than all the teaching seminars in the world!

Unappreciated ministry is hard to keep going ... both sides hurt, those ministering ... and those ministered to! We need to appreciate all those who minister within the congregation ... from smelly diaper changers to faithful janitors ... to board members who serve and do what's best for the church of God, even at the expense of their personal lives – and yes, the pastors, too!

It can be difficult to get people to volunteer to minister ... if we complain about our ministry and make it joyless! Then it's no surprise that no one is anxious to serve! Where ministry is appreciated, there is greater interest in service!

Nothing creates more thanksgiving than giving thanks! People who are thankful tend to be appreciated more than those who are rarely thankful! *Thankfulness breeds thankfulness!*

Thankfulness is at the heart of dynamic worship. The more thankful the heart, the more refreshed the soul. It is also the inspiration of ministry! As thankfulness inspires ministry, it also directs ministry in very practical ways!

Are you a *thank-full* or *thank-empty* person?

CHOICES

Nehemiah 13:1-3

On that day the Book of Moses was read aloud in the hearing of the people and there it was found written that no Ammonite or Moabite should ever be admitted into the assembly of God, because they had not met the Israelites with food and water but had hired Balaam to call a curse down on them. (Our God, however, turned the curse into a blessing.) When the people heard this law, they excluded from Israel all who were of foreign descent.

A Series of Choices

One of the greatest gifts of God outside of salvation is the gift of *choice!* Unlike the animals who operate on a level of instinctive behavior, humans have very few instincts outside of some simple basic ones: *survival, suckling,* and *nurture by food and water.*

Most of the other areas in our lives involve *choices*. Life is really a series of choices ... if we choose wisely, we find joy and self-respect. If we choose unwisely, we suffer sorrows from those poor choices ... some sorrows lasting a lifetime. Even when we choose unwisely ... we can choose to learn from it or become bitter over it!

The ability to choose is ours for the rest of our lives ... it is a powerful and awesome gift ... with a powerful impact on our lives and those closest to us.

Poor Choices

Nehemiah returned and discovered the people had made a series of poor choices, separating the people of Israel from their commitment to God! It was time to call them back to make the right choices *now* ... or suffer the consequences that time and again had led to captivity and bondage!

At one time, God's Word was read to them to let them know what choices they were to make if they wanted God's best! The very basis of wise decisions come from God's Word ... the best source of information! Knowledge sits within our intellect. Wisdom sits within our hearts and will!

No wonder Solomon spent so much time advocating getting *wisdom*, even more than knowledge! Knowledge can impress others with the accumulation and articulation of that knowledge. Wisdom is the ability to take that knowledge and properly apply it by wise choices!

This is why it is possible for some very intelligent people to be so ignorant. And why some very uneducated people can be so wise! Godliness and the commitment of obedience to God's Word is the very *heart of wisdom!* The criteria of healthy choices come from acceptance of God's instructions from His Word ... and the application of those words to our life!

Notice that no one was included in the "assembly of God" unless they were obedient servants of the Word (v. 1)! Was it just the nationality that was excluded here? I think not. Ruth was a Moabitess ... she was accepted by God within the Israelite community. Therefore, the rejection of these people was because of clear evidence that they had helped Israel make choices contrary to God's declared Word. *Get rid of them* was the command! It was not strictly ethnic issues at stake; it was obedience to God's Word that was at stake.

The Only Smart Choice

The only smart choice was to remove the influence of evil from among them! Rather than influencing these evil people for good, just the opposite had happened (as we shall discover later in this chapter around verses 23-27).

The people now faced the choice of breaking off relationships with those who had helped lead them into corruption, a people who had earlier ignored helping Israel in the desert ... in other words, people who only thought of their own needs. Israel didn't need help in becoming more selfish. Human nature already is bent this way. They needed to make a fresh commitment based on the knowledge of God's Word ... in other words: *to choose wisely!*

Nehemiah 13:4-5

Before this, Eliashib the priest had been put in charge of the storerooms of the house of our God. He was closely associated with Tobiah, and he had provided him with a large room formerly used to store the grain offerings and incense and temple articles, and also the tithes of grain, new wine and olive oil prescribed for the Levites, musicians and gatekeepers, as well as the contributions for the priests.

The Unwise Compromise

Eliashib the high priest had compromised himself and all Israel by allowing Tobiah (an ungodly man) to live within the temple structure, something strictly forbidden by God's Word! This compromise had a material or monetary aspect to it! Allowing Tobiah to reside in the temple brought all kinds of trade and goods into Jerusalem and helped the people to acquire more money and goods!

The arrangement may have seemed profitable on the surface but compromising our standards for momentary gain is never a good idea. Sometimes the choices we make to get so much of the world's goods end up compromising our commitment to be faithful to God ... perhaps even in our giving!

In 1 Timothy 6:10, Timothy was instructed by Paul to warn the rich within the church ... in fact, not just the rich but also those who were making the choice to get rich: "... for the love of money is a root of all kinds of evil. Some people, eager for money, have wandered from the faith and *pierced themselves through with many griefs!*" Eliashib did not have his hands twisted behind his back, forced to make this choice ... he chose personal gratification over personal discipline, and the choice would cost him ... but then all choices in life always do *either for good results or evil!* This single compromise by the high priest would have results that would spread throughout all of Jerusalem!

Hardened Hearts

Gradually, as they continued to ignore what was right and choose what they knew to be wrong, the people's hearts got harder and harder until they could rationalize just about any choice they made that was contrary to God's Word!

This still happens today ... the more we choose incorrectly, the easier it gets, and the reduction of guilt becomes a very real consequence! Our hearts become more and more callus toward real righteousness!

The callus hearts of the leaders at this point crept throughout the people of Jerusalem so that they stopped giving ... and thus the Levites and singers could no longer be paid their salaries; they were forced to choose to return to their plots of land and grow grain to subsist on, and so there was no time to prepare for or participate in the temple services!

The choice of one man, the high priest, had now spread throughout the entire city. These were the same people who had celebrated the finished walls in chapter 12 and had made fierce commitments to *never neglect the house of God!* (10:39b "… We will not neglect the house of our God.") Yet, through compromise which bred callousness, they were doing that very thing … *neglecting the house of God* … all because they were now trying to survive financially.

Their unwise choices for prosperity had just the opposite effect! They struggled to stay afloat! God's servants (the Levites) couldn't be paid due to the lack of tithes by the people, and now the Levites had to make a living off the land! They were too busy surviving to do any serving.

When you are too busy for God … you are too busy! Business had become more important than tithes and offerings … so they cleared the storage room for a businessman to live in, thus desecrating the *house of God!* It is interesting to note that Nehemiah wasn't in town during this slip back into compromised living!

Nehemiah 13:6-9

But while all this was going on, I was not in Jerusalem, for in the thirty-second year of Artaxerxes king of Babylon I had returned to the king. Sometime later I asked his permission and came back to Jerusalem. Here I learned about the evil thing Eliashib had done in providing Tobiah a room in the courts of the house of God. I was greatly displeased and threw all Tobiah's household goods out of the room. I gave orders to purify the rooms, and then I put back into them the equipment of the house of God, with the grain offerings and the incense.

Nehemiah's Return

Nehemiah returns only to be shocked by what he finds ... a people who had made all the right decisions when he had left – to a people who now had changed their minds and made choices that were bringing calamity upon them! He knew that soon God's judgment would fall upon them and any hope of being restored would disappear! The only thing to do was to bring correction. Since the corruption had started from the top down ... this is where he begins! We find him going to the *house of God* and throwing out all of the belongings of Tobiah, the businessman!

There came a time when Nehemiah and God constituted the majority vote for action! The scene was archetypical of Jesus throwing the money changers out of the temple! There comes a time to challenge poor choices ... and this was it! Correction involved 3 things:

1. Cleansing the garbage out of the house of God.

2. Purifying again the house of God ... Recognizing the sacredness of the house of God.

3. Restoring the proper equipment and supplies so that the Levites could return to ministry full time!

These were hard choices, but Nehemiah was prepared to make them and act upon them! *That's the secret to success ... act upon your right choices!* It is not enough to want to make the right choice ... we must *do so* and then *act on those choices!* Desire changes very little ... action changes everything!

A Domino Effect

The poor choices while Nehemiah was away had resulted in a domino effect. They had neglected the *house of God*, leading to no income for the Levites, who then had to search for a job to stay alive (farming being their only means of survival), leading to *no word from God* for the people ... and losing sight of God's plan for Jerusalem!

This is the irony of one person's poor choices ... they can have a whole string of effects upon others close to them that bring pain and suffering and even compromise! The choices we make in life are *critical* to both us and those around us! There are *very real consequences to making improper choices!*

Nehemiah 13:10-14

I also learned that the portions assigned to the Levites had not been given to them, and that all the Levites and musicians responsible for the service had gone back to their own fields. So I rebuked the officials and asked them, "Why is the house of God neglected?" Then I called them together and stationed them at their posts.

All Judah brought the tithes of grain, new wine and olive oil into the storerooms. I put Shelemiah the priest, Zadok the scribe, and a Levite named Pedaiah in charge of the storerooms and made Hanan son of Zakkur,

the son of Mattaniah, their assistant, because
they were considered trustworthy. They were
made responsible for distributing the supplies
to their fellow Levites.

Remember me for this, my God, and do not
blot out what I have so faithfully done for the
house of my God and its services.

Refilling the Storeroom

With just one man making again the proper choices, things begin to reverse themselves. Change begins taking place as the people once again make the *right choices!* Soon the people are bringing their tithes back, knowing that the storeroom is empty and Tobiah has left town!

This change allows for the return of the Levites to ministry, a change which would again allow for the people to be challenged to make the right choices based on God's Word! This time however, Nehemiah has four men appointed to make sure the collections are properly handled to prevent another mishap like before! This new concept of mutual accountability helps reduce the possibility of one person's poor choices influencing the rest of God's people!

Nehemiah's Heart of Restoration

It is interesting what Nehemiah prays for at the end of restoring these people to proper choices: *"Remember me for this, O my God!"*

Not *"Reward me ..."* Not *"You people owe me ..."*

Also notice Nehemiah's words in the later part of this verse: *"I have so faithfully done ..."* This is not spiritual pride ... literally translated, the idea is this: *"A quality which accepts obligation and honors it, come what may!"* The idea: Make the right choices no matter how you feel, or what others might say or do! We must understand the importance of properly choosing the right, willing to accept any criticism or mockery ... knowing right choices secure God's favor even when that seems unimportant to others!

Nehemiah 13:15-18

In those days I saw people in Judah treading winepresses on the Sabbath and bringing in grain and loading it on donkeys, together with wine, grapes, figs and all other kinds of loads. And they were bringing all this into Jerusalem on the Sabbath. Therefore, I warned them against selling food on that day. People from Tyre who lived in Jerusalem were bringing in fish and all kinds of merchandise and selling them in Jerusalem on the Sabbath to the people of Judah. I rebuked the nobles of Judah and said to them, "What is this wicked thing you are doing—desecrating the Sabbath day? Didn't your ancestors do the same things, so that our God brought all this calamity on us and on this city? Now you are stirring up more wrath against Israel by desecrating the Sabbath."

Restoring Worship

The people during his absence had also neglected the weekly worship time, instead using the Sabbath as just another day to get richer! This was a very unwise choice spiritually, although it seemed to make sense financially! (Many today still think this way!) Nehemiah takes a firm hand in shutting down the neglect of *God's house on the Sabbath!* ... Somebody must make the choice. Nehemiah does and implements it ... *he has the gates all shut at sundown!* Nehemiah also reminds the leaders of Israel that it was this very practice of ignoring God on the Sabbath that had led to their fathers' captivity ... in other words, you guys have made a very dumb decision ... guess where it will take you if you don't change!?

At first, the traders and businessmen still came, thinking that Nehemiah would give in soon. They waited below the gates for a few weeks, thinking, "*He can't really mean it ... or the people will tire of this old-timer and his commitment to God!*"

They picked the wrong man to bet on! Nehemiah outwaited them! ... Finally, he shouts down to them, "*If you stay there again I myself will come down and lay hands on you!*" They made a wise choice. They quit coming! A mad prophet on God's side can be a scary thing!

Again, success by the right choice ... Nehemiah asks God to remember him for his commitment and stance here! He is only concerned about approval from God! Making the right choices in life is much easier when you know that it is God's approval you should seek, and not man's!

Nehemiah 13:19-29

When evening shadows fell on the gates of Jerusalem before the Sabbath, I ordered the doors to be shut and not opened until the

Sabbath was over. I stationed some of my own men at the gates so that no load could be brought in on the Sabbath day. Once or twice the merchants and sellers of all kinds of goods spent the night outside Jerusalem. But I warned them and said, "Why do you spend the night by the wall? If you do this again, I will arrest you." From that time on they no longer came on the Sabbath. Then I commanded the Levites to purify themselves and ... guard the gates in order to keep the Sabbath day holy.

Remember me for this also, my God, and show mercy to me according to your great love.

Moreover, in those days I saw men of Judah who had married women from Ashdod, Ammon and Moab. Half of their children spoke the language of Ashdod or the language of one of the other peoples, and did not know how to speak the language of Judah. I rebuked them and called curses down on them. I beat some of the men and pulled out their hair. I made them take an oath in God's name and said: "You are not to give your daughters in marriage to their sons, nor are you to take their daughters in marriage for your sons or for yourselves. Was it not because of marriages like these that Solomon king of Israel sinned? Among the many nations there was no king like him. He was loved by his God, and God made him king over all Israel, but even he was led into sin by foreign women. Must we hear now that you too are doing all this terrible wickedness and are being unfaithful to our God by marrying foreign women?"

One of the sons of Joiada son of Eliashib the high priest was son-in-law to Sanballat the Horonite. And I drove him away from me.

Remember them, my God, because they defiled the priestly office and the covenant of the priesthood and of the Levites.

A Pure Identity

The choice to ignore God's call not to marry unbelievers had a devastating effect upon the entire nation and witness of Israel! Nehemiah, as he travels through town, realizes that the people had chosen once again to ignore God's call to not marry unbelievers, and he witnesses the large impact already on the new generation of children born by hearing them speaking in their mothers' native tongues rather than the Jewish tongue of Hebrew!

Why get bent out of shape over this? It meant that the identity of Israel as God's special people was diminishing, and soon there would be no difference between them and the world! The pagan influence was beating out the godly influence; the evidence was in the children's language!

Could there be an important lesson here for us? *Yes!* It is critical that we teach our children *how very important* it is that they identify themselves *with Christ* and not this world. Their language should give away what they are most being influenced by! *Dads and moms* ... we have never lived in a day that *is as important in our commitment to God as today. Your kids will become the future adults of their greatest influences today! What language are they speaking!?* Our choices will have an impact in our children. If we take the *house of God* lightly, they are likely to treat it the same! If we take the *worship of our Lord* as something we do when we have extra time, then our children will reflect that attitude.

If *we speak* evil of our brethren, our children also will. *If we ignore our giving,* they will probably do so, also! *Our children are our greatest gift for the church's continuation. It should drive us* to make choices that reflect our desire to teach them not just the knowledge of God's Word, but show them the wisdom of those choices by practicing that knowledge in our lifestyle! The results can be catastrophic, otherwise!

No More Beating Around the Bush

Nehemiah doesn't beat around the bush ... he takes action. He grabs a few of the men (They were in authority and should have shown the way!) and beat a few of them! Then he pulled their hair out (not the recommended style of discipline today, obviously). Nehemiah reflects a different style of ministry from Ezra, who had the same problem earlier. In Ezra 9:3-4, Ezra sat down *and pulled his own hair out* ... this scared the Jews who then turned their behaviors around.

Nehemiah figures the second time a new tactic should frighten them ... He beats them and tears their hair out instead of his own!

Well, different prophets with different styles ... but both were used effectively by God ... different styles worked because the choices were both the correct one ... be dramatic to prevent a catastrophe!

Solomon serves as an example of someone with great knowledge – but his wisdom was corrupted by ungodly bonds and foreign women. If such a wise man could choose so wrongly, how did they think they could choose the same wrong and escape catastrophe?

Nehemiah 13:30-31

So I purified the priests and the Levites of everything foreign, and assigned them duties, each to his own task. I also made provision for contributions of wood at designated times, and for the first fruits.

Remember me with favor, my God.

The Close of Nehemiah's Ministry

Nehemiah comes now to the close of his ministry, and he reveals his only interest during his lifetime: *to choose what was right*, both for himself and for his brethren whom he had authority over!

Nehemiah knew the proper choices would bring God's blessings upon His people. Those blessings would extend to and influence the world … through the example of a great people serving a great God!

Their constant ability to make the wrong choices led them through cycle after cycle of catastrophe and pain, bondage to bondage!

The same truth applies to us today! Knowing God's Word is not the same as the wisdom of doing God's Word!

Right choices will reward our soul with satisfaction and joy. We will be filled with the knowledge that God will take care of all our needs! *The simple dynamic of choice* will make or break your life. *Choose wisely that you might live!*

Nehemiah's life can be summed up in three things or three choices – a sharp contrast to the three *claims made by the great Caesar,* who said:

"I came ... I saw ... I conquered!"

Nehemiah's life was:

"I cleansed ... I established ... I provided ..."

Nehemiah's life was that of making the proper choices, first for himself and then for his people ... the result was a renewal of God's people and the blessings of God upon them.

We see the importance of choice after Nehemiah is gone when once again a new generation grows up who knows not the Lord, and the cycle of poor choices brings in fresh condemnation and bondage!

The choices we make have consequences to

them, either good or bad. Those consequences rarely affect only our own lives; others are often impacted by them, also. This is also true of good choices. They not only bless us, they impact others by blessing them, too.

The right choices result in cleansing; the wrong choices result in calamity! Be wise, not just smart ... choose correctly and enjoy the fruit of God's blessings and the joy that comes from honoring God!

ABOUT TIM R. BARKER

Reverend Tim R. Barker is the Superintendent of the South Texas District of the Assemblies of God which is headquartered in Houston, Texas.

He is a graduate of Southwestern Assemblies of God University, with a Bachelor of Science degree in General Ministries/Biblical Studies, with a minor in music. He also received a Master of Arts in Practical Theology from SAGU and received his Doctorate of Ministry Degree from West Coast Seminary.

Reverend Barker was ordained by the Assemblies of God in 1989. He began his ministry in the South Texas District in 1984 as youth & music minister and continued his ministry as Pastor, Executive Presbyter (2006 – 2009) and Executive Secretary-Treasurer (2009 – 2011) in the South Texas District, where he served until his election as the South Texas District Superintendent in 2011.

By virtue of his district office, Reverend Barker is a member of the District's Executive Presbytery and the General Presbytery of the General Council of the Assemblies of God, Springfield, Missouri. He is a member of the Executive Board of Regents for Southwestern Assemblies of God University, Waxahachie, Texas and SAGU-American Indian College, Phoenix, Arizona. He is a member of the Board of Directors of Pleasant Hills Children's Home, Fairfield, Texas, as well as numerous other boards and committees.

Reverend Barker and his wife, Jill, married in 1983, have been blessed with two daughters. Jordin and her husband, Stancle Williams, who serves as the South Texas District Youth Director. Abrielle and her husband, Nolan McLaughlin, are church planters of Motion Church in San Antonio. The Barkers have four grandchildren, Braylen, Emory and Landon Williams and Kingston McLaughlin.

His unique style of pulpit ministry and musical background challenges the body of Christ, with an appeal that reaches the generations.

Contact Tim

Pastor Tim would love to hear from you. You can reach him at www.TimBarker.ag.

Click on Ask Pastor Tim for more information.